Great Sex, Christian Style
All the tips, history, religion, and humor your sex life can handle.

What Readers Say About GSCS

"OMG it's funny. Let your wife know that I do name changes!" – Attorney JD Young

"As a clinical psychologist, I've asked Senior Pastors and Youth Pastors to talk to their folks about sex...with almost no success. *Great Sex, Christian Style* will help couples improve their communication and relationships." – Dr. E.E. "Grif" Griffith

"*Great Sex, Christian Style* by Ned Pelger is one man's honest pursuit of sexual happiness for the God-loving universe. With humor and soul, Pelger explores the sexual wake of Christianity, communicating insightful navigations and scholarly musings on centuries-old practice and teachings. *Great Sex* challenges Christians and non-Christians alike to question what they thought they knew about the Bible and sex. And it's a perfect stocking stuffer for that hard-to-please mother-in-law." – Chris DiCicco, author *So My Mother, She Lives in the Clouds*

"A great combination of historical facts, anatomy and practical sex advice for dummies...reads like a cold beer on a hot summer day." – A Bosnian immigrant who has seen the worst of life and now strives to enjoy the best

"Growing up in a conservative Christian family, this was not a conversation we had at home or in church. In fact, it wasn't even a permitted topic for internal reflection. I married my husband as a 21-year-old virgin who wasn't completely sure of the workings of my own anatomy.

Bible college perhaps prepared me for submission (giant eye roll) but not a thoughtful and intentional approach to sex. I appreciate Ned's honesty and forthrightness in touching a subject that few are brave enough to confront. I admire the way Ned did it in an approachable, humble way, which made it less awkward for the reader." – A thirtysomething mom who has three kids and runs a business

"Until I started reading this book I was happily ignorant with regard to the depth of my selfishness and laziness as a lover. So, thanks for that." – A computer programmer married for many years

"I would have never written this book. I don't have the guts. I don't even agree with everything, but I do think you should read it. It will make you think. It will improve your marriage and it will help you understand God better." – Pastor of a large, growing church

"Thoughtful, original, and leavened with (sometimes outrageous) humor." – an attorney husband and physician wife (the couple every contractor tries to avoid)

"Ned Pelger does the most important thing an author can do: he writes honestly about scary things. And he's funny about it." – A young husband in Barcelona

"WOW. Ned is up to his old humorous self and tackles a forbidden topic in most Christian circles with gusto and amazing intimacy. I never knew a Bible study could be so fun, exciting...and graphic!! I don't agree with all of his conclusions, but I do agree wholeheartedly with Ned that love, grace, and respect must be the foundation for all relationships. Way to go, Ned, for laying it on the line and giving us an engineer's perspective on one of God's greatest creations!" – A 60 something church worker and recovering banker

"What leads one to write a book like this? Perhaps 40 years of monogamous Christian sex?" – An inquiring mind wants to know

"I realize I spent way too much time in my first 40 years on the odd chapters (how to do sex better) and really only found great and soul satisfying sex the last twenty years when I worked much harder on the even chapters. It isn't the sex that makes the relationship, it's the relationship that makes the sex. Feel free to use my name. I doubt too many people will ever see it." – Michael R Bingeman, CPA, who is just glad he found a woman who lets him see her naked (and friend of Ned's since 1960)

"I'm reading this and laughing my buttocks off (or words to that effect)!" – former Vietnam sniper and current owner of large tech company

"*GSCS* examines marital sex without apology. That approach will be very freeing for people, particularly for those who grew up in religious surroundings. What I appreciated the most, though, was Ned's continual challenge to the reader to take their questions and concerns about sex and behavior to God. Christians always talk about having a personal relationship with Christ yet we often don't live it. Christian leaders often allow their parishioners to remain at a childish faith level because we establish (and enforce) the rules, boundaries, and consequences for them." – Pastor of a small, growing church

"At first glance, Ned's book appears to be about sex and indeed it is quite intimate. But upon further review, it also seems to me that the book is about our relationship with God, our relationships with each other, and what great joys can be found therein. The Song of Solomon section reminded me of the joke about a guy doing an ink blot Rorschach test with a psychiatrist. The first picture he sees a woman's breasts, then a woman bent over, then a vulva and so on. The shrink says, 'Sir, you seem to have an obsession with sex.' The guys replies, 'Me? You're the one showing the dirty pictures!'" – Penn Ketchum, Founder and Partner, Penn Cinema

"Very well done! Who doesn't like to read about sex? Great research throughout the book. A superb and incomparable Biblical perspective on sex, including how-to techniques. Audaciously explicit. Discretion is advised if considering as a coffee table book!" – Jay Polansky, PE, partner Professional Design and Construction

"Finally a book that takes the lid of the awkwardness of sexual discussion—a book that both sexes can engage in. You'll laugh, you'll cry—you'll get it on!" – Erik and Jackie Schouten, entrepreneurs married 27 years

"Ned is sick. He sent me a review copy of this book knowing I am dyslexic. I spent weeks trying to get past the first paragraph. There are not enough photos!" – A former customer in his late 60's who sold his business for a huge price, none of which came to Ned (as it rightfully should have)

"Quite novel and fun, though likely controversial by those much more serious and scholarly than myself; that's probably good for a book." – Dave Williams, Founder Sechan Electronics

"A surprisingly wry approach to a topic with a high squirm quotient, *Great Sex, Christian Style* is part marriage manual, part philosophical tract. But it's also a deeply felt, personal account of the author's journey from judgment to acceptance, offered to the reader with love." – D.W. Gregory, playwright and author of *Radium Girls* and *Salvation Road*

"As an engineer, I'm used to being told to loosen up...which is essentially what this book told me. While I didn't agree with everything, my convictions were challenged and that's a good thing. And while my wife and I have a good sex life, I'm encouraged that it can be even better." – A civil engineer with a heart

"Ned Pelger delivers a clear, concise, and compelling message in his naturally humorous writing style. He goes 'deep with the little things' that can enrich your sex experiences...and maybe your faith and marriage. Be ready for a few jaw-dropping moments. I strongly encourage anyone to buy *Great Sex, Christian Style*. Oh, and remember to make your bed!" – Stan Zeamer Chairman of Utility Keystone Trailer Sales

"Sorry it took so long to get back to you, but I needed a week to recover after trying all the positions from Ned's book! It's one of the most hilarious compendiums of adult toys, positions, and the affected human anatomy I have ever seen. I laughed so hard I had an orgasm. This is a must read for every marriage counselor, rabbi, priest, and newlywed couple. Ned's wife is a saint for putting up with him…I know mine is, especially after I showed her page 72. What a titillating journey through the silliness of sex and relationships." – Ben Samberg, RA owner, Lancaster Architectural Works

Great Sex, Christian Style

All the tips, history, religion, and humor your sex life can handle.

by Ned Pelger, PE

ATA Publishing Company

ATA Publishing Company
Website: www.ATAPub.com
Contact email address (for permissions questions and other inquiries):
info@ATAPub.com

Edited by Kathrin Herr, The Writing Mechanic.
Formatted and Designed by Kathrin Herr, The Writing Mechanic,
thewritingmechanic.net.

Cover Photo purchased from Shutterstock.com.
Standard License. # 618101087.

Author Photo by LuAnn Rohrer Photography.

Published by ATA Publishing Company, 507 W. 28th Division Hwy,
Lititz, PA 17543.

The publisher does not control or assume responsibility for author or
third-party websites or their content.

GREAT SEX, CHRISTIAN STYLE

ISBN: 978-0-9624569-0-9

Printed in the USA by Create Space print-on-demand.
Also available in e-book format through Amazon Kindle Direct
Publishing.

Dedication

To Debby, a reserved person who hates that I've written this book.

We've been together since we were 17, never broken up, never committed murder (though there have been periods of planning), had kids and grandkids, and lived with successes and failures. You've made life joyful for me. And since you'll probably never read this (and certainly never give me the satisfaction of knowing you did), the sex has been marvelous.

I'm so glad you and I worked together to create our little piece of God's magnificent tapestry. I wouldn't have wanted to do it with anyone else.

Introduction 1

1. Tips of the Trade for Great Sex 7

2. Getting Lucky in Ancient Times 33

3. Oral Sex: Let's Talk About It 65

4. God Talks Sex 85

5. Aphrodisiacs: Who-ahhh! 97

6. I Just Want to be Biblical 117

7. Getting Handy: Fingers as Sex Toys 143

8. Sexual Epiphanies 159

9. The Ins and Outs of Intercourse 169

10. Romance: A Life Well Lived 195

11. Toys, Stories & Games 213

Introduction

I'm much better at sex than my wife. I achieve orgasm every single time. She only does sometimes.[1]

Years ago I obsessed over this dilemma. Now I know better. I wrote this book to help you know better: how to better enjoy sex, to learn God's views about sex, and how to not be a jerk about sex.

If you believe in God, perhaps you believe as I do that God made all people sacred. He created us in his image and has important plans for each of us. God made procreation happen in a funny, sweaty, rolling-around manner that seems anything but sacred. Sex shows God's sense of humor. Hippopotamuses and giraffes do a pretty good job at that too.

Do you remember when you first learned about sex? Do you remember being incredulous? Years ago, I took four of our female sheep to a neighbor's ram for

---

[1] Are you reading this footnote to check Debby's rate of orgasm? If so, "Don't worry your pretty little head about that." This note is to give credit to Ron White, who used a similar joke in his comedy routine, which helped inspire me to write this book.

breeding. My eight-year-old daughter rode along with me to the farm. We let the ewes into the pasture and they scurried down to the far end.

The ram was at the opposite end of the field. His nose went up in the air, he caught a whiff of sweet, and he sprinted across the field. He immediately mounted one of the ewes (not much foreplay for sheep) and did his job.

My daughter was watching all this, and I realized I had a chance to teach. I explained in general terms that what she just saw was part of the circle of life, and that's where the baby lambs will come from. She looked at me and said, "Do you and Mom do that?"

I stammered, "Uh, well, yeah. Pretty much."

That was the first and last question she ever asked me about sex. I told that story to a shy friend years ago, and he told me he was going to be sure to raise his children in such a way that they would never ask him that question.

I wrote this book to help my readers explore the fun and beauty of sex while learning more about God. I'll warn you from the onset: I'm an all-in Christian, not an armchair traveler. The Bible tells us to be strong and courageous. Fear, laziness, and selfishness are the enemy. If you think Christian sex consists of avoiding sin and judging others, you're in for a long ride here. But, if those are your beliefs, perhaps it's the only long ride you'll get.

I love the theology of Dietrich Bonhoeffer. A biographer sums it up with the following quote:

> Being a Christian is less about cautiously avoiding sin than about courageously and actively doing God's will.[2]

So we're going real-world in this book—not gentle theories. The practical information I provide will make some of you blush. I admit, that fact makes me much happier than it should, but that's my problem.

Please take everything I write (or anybody writes) with healthy skepticism. Perhaps I can point you in a direction that works for you. Hopefully I can make you laugh. I certainly make myself laugh.

For example, my high school yearbook lists my likes as "sex and money" and my dislikes as "promiscuity and materialism." That still makes me laugh and shows the weirdo that is me. From that kooky dichotomy, I organize this book:

---

[2] Eric Metaxas, *Bonhoeffer: Pastor, Martyr, Prophet, Spy: a Righteous Gentile vs. the Third Reich* (Nashville, TN, Thomas Nelson, 2010), p. 486.

1. **Odd numbered chapters**: Physical Sex Tips (the practical)
2. **Even numbered chapters:** Bible Study and Emotional Analysis on Sex and Marriage (the theoretical)

If you just care about the sex tips, read the odd numbered chapters. If you only care about Biblical analysis and not sex—in which case, I "put pity on you"—read the even chapters. My hope is that you want to have great sex and know God's view on it. If that's you, read the book straight through.

You may wonder—as does my wife—why I wrote this book. The answer is simple: I wrote it because no one else has. Pastors can't; they'd get fired. Famous Christian authors don't because Christian book stores don't carry controversy. I wrote it because somebody needed to.

I'm a layman, not a theologian, scholar, or sex therapist. Christianity has a wonderful tradition of layman writing, from John Bunyan to C.S. Lewis.[3] I hope to honor that tradition.

---

[3] John Bunyan wrote Pilgrim's Progress in the 1600s, one of the most read books ever written. If you haven't read it, you should. C.S. Lewis wrote dozens of amazing books and essays.

Why should you read my book? For one, you and your spouse can cultivate a thrilling love relationship with the tips, tricks, and knowledge I share in these pages. Competence, silliness, enthusiasm, and kindness all matter greatly when it comes to sex. I want to help you develop those attributes and continually improve your sex life. I will challenge you to get out of your comfort zone and learn to innovate.

I also want you to learn God's views about sex and marriage...even if they don't jive with what you've been taught. You'll discover that it's not just a list of simple rules.

If God wanted us to live by simple rules, the Bible would be about 20 pages long. Know that living a God-focused life will require courage and faith—not simply blind rule following. The same will be true with your marriage.

I'm a practical guy. We're going to cover specifics of what to do and how to do it. We're going to push the boundaries of our understanding. We're going to get laid! So let's get right into some practical facts that will get you feeling better than you ever have.

Chapter 1

Tips of the Trade for Great Sex

For most folks, sex happens quickly: A few kisses, some random rubbing, then insert and pound away till the man finishes and the woman, well, doesn't. It's not surprising that this is the norm. That's the way it works with dogs and sheep and donkeys: sex that scratches the itch—at least for the male of the species—slams, bams, and thank-you-ma'ams.

If that's your sexual style, you need this book. Perhaps you're not such a Neanderthal and have boned up on the concept of foreplay. Generally, men can be ready for sex quickly. A flash of thigh on a windy street and most are ready for action.

Women tend to need more time. While this book will help both women and men enjoy sex more, men need more help. We are often mostly clueless about satisfying our wives. I'll try to provide those clues.

Chapter 1: Tips of the Trade for Great Sex

Unfortunately, I'll need to keep qualifying statements such as the above throughout this book. Sex varies so much between people. That makes every generalization wrong (including this one). Nevertheless, trends exist, and we can learn from them.

For example, the generalization "Great sex takes time" is mostly true. One of the many movie lines that rattles around in my head is from *Love at First Bite*, a 1979 comedy in which Count Dracula says, in all his Transylvanian charm, "With you...nev-ah a kwik-kee...all-vays...a long-gee."

How do you get from a quickie to a longie? How do you move from somewhat unsatisfying sex to amazing, intimate sex? Well, how do you get better at anything? You take an interest in the activity, learn about what works for others, and then practice.

Debby and I were married for many years and had what we thought was a reasonably good sex life. Then I read *Intended for Pleasure: Sex Technique and Sexual Fulfillment in Christian Marriage* and picked up some valuable pointers. [4] Unfortunately, it is 285 pages long and written with all the charm of a high school health class taught by an evangelist.

---

[4] Ed Wheat, MD and Gaye Wheat, *Intended for Pleasure: Sex Techniques and Sexual Fulfillment in Christian Marriage* (Grand Rapids, MI, Revell, 1997).

What did I learn that made sex immediately better? Let's spell it together: C-L-I-T-O-R-I-S. Why all this fuss about the clitoris? The clitoris has almost 8,000 nerve endings (about twice as many as the penis) in a spot the size of a pea. But it's more than just a super sensitive place. To put it bluntly, the clitoris is where female orgasms come from.

Clitoris Hunting

For men, the most important anatomical fact you will ever learn is the exact location of the clitoris. Found one inch above the entrance to the vagina, the clitoris has a pea sized head located at the end of a short shaft about one-inch in length. Unlike the penis, the clitoris doesn't contain an opening for urination. That urethra opening is located between the vaginal opening and the clitoris.

An astounding number of men are clitoris-clueless and never get their spouse to orgasm. If you're not sure of the exact location, find it during your next sexual escapade. Go on a hunting trip.

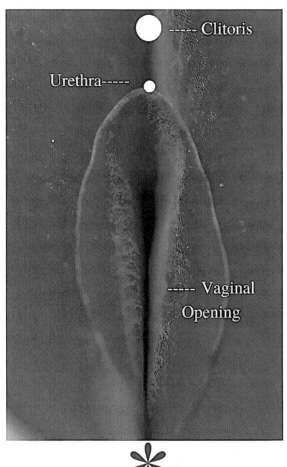

As delicate and beautiful as a rose... (Anus as depicted by Kurt Vonnegut, Jr).

But before you start this excursion, let's make sure you've got the right supplies. You need good lubrication, and options abound. KY Jelly remains an old standby. It is water based, cheap, and you can buy it at the grocery store. A more specialized silicon lube, such as Passion Lube, lubricates longer and feels less sticky. You can buy Passion Lube online through Amazon and at some drugstores.

Avoid oil based lubes like Vaseline. The oil clogs pores, limiting the vagina's ability to cleanse itself and inviting infection. Oil lubes can also damage latex condoms, and they are sticky and gross. So pony up and get some decent personal lubricant to set for the ready on your nightstand.

Now, back to clitoris hunting. After some preliminaries (moving toward sexual arousal) take a well lubricated finger and find the vagina opening. We should all know where that is. Then move up the body slightly, just an inch or so, and feel that little shaft. It'll feel like you're running your finger over a coffee stirrer—or maybe a straw if she's excited.

Gently touch the clitoris shaft and head. Go with a slow, gentle, lightly caressing motion. Be careful with this super-sensitive spot. You will likely feel it enlarge a bit (though it doesn't on all women) and get harder (kind of like a penis).

Female Orgasms

While the clitoris has similarities to the penis, the next most important lesson, after finding it, is to realize how different it is from the penis. Masturbation for most men is about squeezing hard and going fast. So men naturally assume it's the same for women. It's not. Since there are so many more nerve endings in the clitoris than the penis, touch gently and vary the motion.

Another way women tend to be different from men is that when you hit the right motion and frequency on the clitoris (producing moans, words, hip motion, or increased natural lubrication) keep going exactly the way you are. Don't change a thing; hang in there to orgasm and beyond.

A man masturbating would likely go harder and faster as orgasm approaches. Resist the urge to do that with a woman. Remember, when you hit the right spot and motion near orgasm, don't change a thing.

For most women, clitoral stimulation will be the easiest mode to orgasm, so that's a great place to start. Hopefully you'll have years to experiment with other options. Some women climax from nipple play alone and a rare few can orgasm just by thinking (I'm glad I don't have that superpower...I wouldn't get much else done in life).

Learning the information above, which occurred decades into our marriage, greatly improved our sex life. Learning how to please each other seems simple but often isn't. Many people struggle to talk about sex. Even with their spouses, folks are too embarrassed to talk.

Many married couples go decades having lousy sex until they finally get comfortable enough to talk through their issues. With some adjustments, these couples start having the best sex of their lives, even though their 40- or 50-year-old bodies wouldn't win any beauty contests.

It got much better for them—and for Debby and me—and it can get better for you too. Don't obsess about what could have happened in the past. Understand that the past shaped you (good and bad) for where you are now.

Don't worry about what may happen in the future. You only have this present moment. You get to choose to make things better, to make things worse, or to do nothing. Choose better.

Searching for that First Orgasm?

But what if you've never had an orgasm? Many women haven't. To start, lose the guilt and disdain. Take up this great orgasm adventure. Remember, sex should be joyful and fun—a gift from God.

Like many of God's gifts, though, misuse abounds. If you've had sexual trauma in your past—and so many have—please consider professional counseling. It isn't something that simply gets better with time. It is a big deal. Don't let anyone tell you otherwise. Don't minimize the importance of it.

Past sexual trauma generally needs to be addressed and worked through over time. You will be amazed at how much your life improves if you have the courage to face past abuse.

If you're a woman who doesn't generally (or ever) experience orgasm, you probably have feelings of shame and guilt—as does your husband. Plus, you probably blame each other on some level. Start by working on the God-ordained practice of forgiveness.

Forgive your spouse and forgive yourself. In your daily prayers, mention this forgiveness specifically, almost as if you are trying to talk yourself into believing it. Forgiveness is rarely a one-time affair.

Jesus, who puzzled his followers with so many of his teachings, was clear about forgiveness: As you forgive others is how you will be forgiven.[5] For past sexual disappointments with your spouse, forgive. Remember to forgive yourself as well.

---

[5] Matthew 6:4

Vow to each other that you will start fresh. Learn to make love without anxiety or criticism. This aspect of marriage is the two of you versus everybody else. Build the special closeness, both inside and outside the bedroom. We'll discuss romance and intimacy later, but that will be central to the improvement of your sex life.

Getting back to orgasms, understand that a man's orgasm tends to be a mechanical event. Rub that penis and ejaculation likely follows. It doesn't much matter who does the rubbing.

Female orgasms aren't so automatic. Generally, the conditions must be right. Things like a romantic atmosphere, a loving, competent partner, and good lubrication up the odds for climax.

Try an orgasm training camp. Don't make it a grim march to climax; make it a playful and fun exercise. Start with a few days of just exploring each other's bodies with gentle caresses and massage.

Don't climax or even focus on private parts. Just get naked and talk to each other about what feels good. Use lots of lubrication. Do it for as long as it is pleasing. Giggles are good here...just don't point and giggle.

Then, try some sessions more focused on the genitalia. A great position for this exploration is the man sitting in bed with his back against the headboard. The woman sits between his legs, facing the same way, and leaning back against the man.

From this position, the man can easily caress breasts, thighs and other white meat. The woman can give some direction here for what feels good and what doesn't.

Don't go for an orgasm yet, just comfortably caress and learn. Again, make sure to use lots of lubrication. Keep the scene and the touches light.

At some point, getting close to orgasm won't be enough and you'll want to go ahead and finish. Don't focus on it or make it the goal. Relax and enjoy the process. Consider mutual pleasure to keep things from getting too one-sided.

Also, since many of us had our first orgasm by our own hand, refer to the sections on female stimulation and masturbation in chapter 7. No one knows better what feels good to you than you.

Finally, don't make orgasms the Holy Grail of your sex life. Some folks will never have an orgasm but can still have satisfying sex lives. The relationship, the connection, and the love weave together to make sex amazing. If it doesn't end with a bang, a nice, long whimper can be nice too.

Lack of Interest in Sex

Did you ever think about why you have sex? We seem to be able to break it down into two main reasons:

1. Your hormones drive it.
2. Your partner wants to.

If you both are in category one, schedule the countdown. If one of you is in category one and the other in two, well, that's a normal situation.

Debby and I got married when I was between my sophomore and junior years in college. In the locker room after wrestling practice, a teammate said to me, "Wow, it must be great to be married, to get it anytime you want it."

I asked him at our 35th class reunion what he thought of that comment now after 30 years of marriage. He just laughed and shook his head. We agreed it's not quite as simple as "getting it anytime you want it."

In marriage, one partner will always have a lesser libido, and it's not always the woman. The person with less sexual drive has power, having the ability to withhold sex from the more motivated partner. Of course, the motivated one can badger, pout, and push to get his or her own way.

Jesus tells us how to behave in this situation, though none of us actually wants to obey. Jesus commands us to not strive for our own way but to give in love to one another. If both partners in a marriage are striving to give in love, beautiful things happen. Practice the discipline of not pushing to get your own way and experience the joy that follows.

Contemplate power and kindness in your sex life. What power do you have? How do you use that power? In what ways could you give up that power by acting with kindness? These questions challenge you in ways that can transform your life.

Even if resentment runs deep, forgiveness goes far to solve the problem resentment causes. Of course, there are people and situations from which you must flee. Jesus doesn't tell us to be abused; he tells us not to be jerks.

I deal in more detail with anger or resentment in the chapter titled, "Aphrodisiacs: Who-ahh!" I'm fairly certain this will be the only sex book you come across that classifies forgiveness and the rest of the Fruits of the Spirit as aphrodisiacs. If the brain is the most important sex organ, the Fruits of the Spirit are the best aphrodisiac.[6]

---

[6] Love, joy, peace, patience, kindness, goodness, faithfulness, gentleness, and self-control (Galatians 5:22).

Finally, if you are always feeling guilty about lack of sex drive, please don't let my words pound you down. Turn to the Lord in prayer and ask God what you should do. It's God's direction you should follow.

Carnal Calisthenics

Before we jump off into premature ejaculation, let's cover an exercise that helps both men and women better enjoy sex. The PC muscle exercises—often called Kegels and pronounced KAY-gulls—are performed by squeezing or contracting the muscles that stop the flow of urine.

As you contract the PC muscle, you can feel your rectum tighten and your genitals pull back. Try it as you read. (No one will notice.) Just squeeze like you are peeing by your car on the side of a highway and have to stop because a police car pulls up. That happens to other people, right?

As you squeeze, try not to tighten your legs or back. Focus on those pelvic floor muscles that go from your genitals to your rectum. All the muscles work together as one.

As you pretend to stop the flow of urine, you will also feel your rectum tighten like you are "pinching off a loaf" or trying to avoid flatulence. If you're feeling adventurous, see if you can feel tightening around a finger inserted into the vagina or anus.

You know the exercise now, but why should you bother to do it on a regular basis? Women, your vagina is not particularly sensitive to touch but is sensitive to pressure—one of the only parts of the body like this. As the vagina squeezes a penis (the squeeze strengthens when the PC muscles are stronger), the pleasure of sex increases substantially for both partners.

For both men and women, the intensity of orgasms increases substantially when these muscles are in better shape (and—bonus—urinary incontinence improves). Kegels make the vagina feel tighter and the penis last longer and work better. If you want better sex, do Kegels.

Like all exercise programs, begin with moderation and build up slowly:

1. **Start with "Quick Pumps."** A few times a day, squeeze and release 10 times. Build it up to 25 or 50 times over a few days or weeks. You may eventually work up to 100.
2. After you work up to 25 quick pumps, move on to **"Slow Squeeze and Slow Release."** Take a few seconds to go from relaxed to fully contracted. Then, hold a couple seconds and slowly relax. As your muscle control improves, go from 10 to 25 of these.

3. After you can do 25 slow contractions, move to **"Thirds."** Start fully relaxed, then slowly squeeze to about 1/3 of full contraction and hold for a moment. Then, squeeze harder to 2/3 of full contraction. Then go to full contraction. Hold for a few seconds and then move back down through that cycle.

You can do them in bed, while driving, while doing some other type of workout, when working, or while you read (that means now). This is the perfect multi-tasking exercise. If you want better sex and stronger orgasms, start doing Kegels immediately.

Premature Ejaculation

Now let's move on to the most common male problem in sex: Premature Ejaculation (PE). If you're a Minute Man but not fighting for your country's independence, pay attention.

I remember all too clearly my early sexual encounters where I came before even getting inside or within the first few strokes. It was so embarrassing.

Of course, as a young man, I was ready for action again in short order so it wasn't a total failure. The next rounds tended to go better. When I learned more about sex, though, I realized I could practice some techniques to delay my ejaculation.

I'm a numbers guy. The technique that always works for me is to count backward from 100 to zero, then up to 100 in Spanish. That couple minutes of focusing on something other than how good intercourse feels helps me last as long as I want. (By the way, I *don't* count out loud.)

You may find success reciting Bible verses or poetry in your head, or use the old standby of thinking about baseball. Here's a story that illustrates the concept:

An old guy walks a donkey on a lead rope down the road, and the donkey decides to stop. The man tries to drag, push and whip the donkey into moving again, but it doesn't get that donkey moving. So the old guy picks up a handful of gravel and feeds it to the donkey. The donkey chews, showing those big teeth and trying to get that nasty tasting gravel out of his mouth. As he chews, the donkey begins walking forward again.

A stranger asks the old man, "Do you mean to tell me that feeding that donkey gravel made him walk?" The old timer responds, "Nah, it chust changed the current of his thinking."

I'm the jackass in the story. Counting changes my thinking and allows me to keep going during intercourse. When I distract myself at the beginning, I go from a sex sprinter to more leisurely enjoying the activity.

Thinking about baseball doesn't work for me, but counting does, and one or the other might work for you. Experiment and determine if a couple minutes of unmindful thinking works for you. If not, what else can you do?

As I studied literature on the subject, I found a few things that seem a good idea to avoid. Desensitizing creams don't seem helpful and have the added disadvantage of potentially desensitizing your spouse's pleasure.

Medication may have lousy side effects. Many sex therapists write about the squeeze technique—getting close to ejaculation and then pinching hard on the end of the penis. From what I've read, it works for the short term but rarely solves the real problem. And who wants the end of their penis pinched? Unless you do...then have at it.

The technique that does seem to work for tough cases of PE could be given the name "Being Mindful About Your Penis." Rather than thinking about baseball or road kill or counting in a foreign language, the man should pay full attention to how his penis feels.

If you describe your penis as feeling "hard," you are describing what your hand feels when you touch your penis. "Tingly" or "throbbing" or "exploding" are examples of words that describe how your penis feels during intercourse.

The common method for lasting longer during sex involves trying to minimize the sensation that feels good. The man may thrust less, the woman may feel like she needs to lie there quietly so as not to over-stimulate him. That's a poor recipe for fun.

If that is your current approach, try being mindful instead. Pay more attention to how your penis feels. Put your feeling on a scale from 0 to 10 with 0 being absolutely no arousal and 10 being orgasmic.

Now it's hand job time—not the normal rush-to-finish hand job, but a *slow* job. If your spouse is a good sport, have her lube up her hand and your penis and start caressing.

Most men with PE go from a 3 to 10 quickly. That's what you want to avoid. Work your way up to a 6 or 7, then back it off. Work back up and back it off again. Have fun with it. Talk about what number you're at and how you feel. Eventually, try to stay at a 6 or 7 for 15 or 20 minutes. Then, finish the deed, and be sure to offer to return the favor.

The man should learn to recognize the point of no return. Let's call that point a 9. When you get to a 9, nothing short of an amputated finger will keep you from ejaculating.[7] You want to be able to recognize when you get to 8 and 8.5, because once you hit 9, you will immediately move to 10 and "spill your seed upon the ground."[8]

The woman should probably stop caressing the penis when you tell her you are at an 8 and massage something else. Give the man 30 seconds to move back from 8 to 5, then start again. The word for this process is "edging," as in "getting close to the edge of the cliff, then stepping back."

By the way, don't worry about erections in this process. You may be hard from 3 and up, or you may only really get hard at 8. It doesn't matter. The less you think about your erection, the better.

After several sessions of hand-calibrating your penis, you will want to try to go live. Make sure plenty of lubrication is involved, take your time, and pay attention to how your penis feels. If you get to 8, you may want to pull out for a bit and make love in some other way. Change things up. Have fun. Remember to breathe and relax. Try some deep breathing. You can do this.

One last thing: If you struggle with PE on occasion or all the time, stop apologizing. One of the things

---

[7] Read the Father Sergius story by Leo Tolstoy if you want to truly understand this reference…or me.

[8] Genesis 38:8-10

partners find the most annoying is shame and apologizing after the quick squirt.[9] It happened. You didn't try to make it happen and you're not a terrible person…well, you may be…but not because of that. In a nutshell, don't make it all about you.

Criticism Destroys Intimacy

Want to know my guide for criticism? If I want to criticize, I don't. If I have carefully thought the situation over and really don't want to deliver the criticism but feel the Holy Spirit guiding me to criticize, then I do. And remember, as Debby often tells me, "Timing is everything." (I'm never altogether sure what she means by that, but I hope I'm learning.)

An example of criticism in our marriage involved Premenstrual Syndrome (PMS). When I was a younger man, I tracked the first day of Debby's period and the one week prior to the onset of PMS in my Day-Timer calendar. I used a little red frowny face for the period and a black one for PMS.

It was a good reminder for me when I got home from work and the feces hit the fan. I'd remember, *This is a chemical reaction that isn't necessarily my*

---

[9] Paul Joannides, *Guide to Getting It On: A Book About the Wonders of Sex* (Oregon: Goofy Foot Press, 2014), p. 731. This is a fantastic book with comprehensive detail and wonderful humor. Some Christians, though, may be put off by the range of topics, the voice, or the length.

*fault…*unless it was. Debby rarely made excuses and never apologized, but one time she said, "Do you think I like being this way?"

When PMS was intense for Debby, sex was particularly annoying to her. I often acted the jerk and pushed for sex anyway. Looking back, though, sex during these times wasn't really much good for either of us. One of the advantages of age is that sex drives aren't quite as intense. The ability to wait a day or two makes our whole relationship, including the sex, better.

Some women feel as though they are out of control when they experience PMS. That tends to present itself as feelings of anger, peevishness, and resentment. The wise man plans and executes a strategy to support his spouse during this time. He *decides* not to criticize. It's a great time to practice the discipline of not taking things personally. Besides, we both know you probably deserve much worse.

Kissing and Massage

If you want great sex, kiss and massage often. Both show love, but don't forget that competence matters too. When someone tongues like a Roto-Rooter or slobbers like a Saint Bernard, kissing quickly goes from erotic to gross. Don't do that.

Kissing can be gentle or intense. Either person can control the kiss, or the control can go back and forth. Kissing should be intensely personal.

Ask your partner to kiss you the way she or he likes. That's a good place to start—and come back to from time to time. Strive to build increased intimacy with your partner year after year.

Have you noticed that most women dance better than men? It's another generalization that has plenty of exceptions, but it holds some truth. Like dancing, most women tend to be better at kissing than men.

Here's some advice for wives: If your husband kisses like he's trying to prime a pump, consider teaching him to kiss differently. In attempt to modify any husband's behavior, you may want to use the following steps:

1. First, **tell him.** Use words. Tell him in English. *No hable Español.* Unless he does *hable Español*, then that's probably fine.
2. Then, **tell him again** a few more times. Understand this great, not-so-secret secret: men are dense.
3. Finally, when you're telling him, **do it without contempt or judgment**. You'd be surprised if you knew how tender his heart really is and how much your criticism hurts

him. Just don't expect him to let you know; he might not know himself.

One way or another, your kissing should continue to be a source of pleasure and play. Now let's consider massage. Almost everyone likes a good massage. Our tight muscles relax with the right pressure, allowing more overall relaxation. Here are some massage tips:

1. Consider the various **types of massage** and decide which ones you want to give and/or your partner wants to receive:
   a. Back massage
   b. Foot massage
   c. Hand massage
   d. Scalp massage
   e. Neck and shoulder massage
   f. Leg and butt massage
   g. Full body massage
2. Consider **sources of friction** and ways to lessen it for a more pleasurable experience:
   a. Over the clothing
   b. Hands on raw skin
   c. Hands on powdered skin (Baby Powder is just cornstarch. You may have some in your kitchen.)
   d. Hands on oiled skin with heated massage oil, baby oil, or another oil option

3. **Go slow**. The most common massage error—after not even trying—is moving your hands too fast. Go with slow, firm pressure that moves the muscle under the skin.

4. **Don't cause too much pain.** A bit of discomfort often occurs in a good massage, but it shouldn't really hurt. Ask your partner to tell you what feels good and what just hurts.

5. **Use all your tools**: fingers, palms, heels of your hands, forearms, a tennis ball, massage sticks, or massage vibrators. Each of these can produce great results. To keep from making yourself too tired, mix things up. Some light punches and Karate chops also add fun variety...just don't do that when you're angry.

6. **Be careful with bones and joints**. Don't push directly on the spine and be gentle at all joints.

7. **Cool down with light touch strokes**, perhaps using only fingernails.

8. If you're a visual learner, **go to YouTube** and type in "How to give" any of the items listed in #1.

9. **Experiment and have fun.**

To build a wonderful relationship with your spouse, give massages. By the way, make sure that, "Let me give you a massage," doesn't always lead to sex. Occasionally practice the "Art of Self-Restraint."

Not that I follow this advice...but I'm sure you should.

Chapter 2

Getting Lucky in Ancient Times

To understand any book, you must understand the culture in which it was written. I love reading Dickens in part because I am fascinated with the history of the early Industrial Age. By history, I don't mean memorizing dates and heads of state; I mean the social history of how people *actually lived*. Dickens comes alive when you have a better sense of how families functioned, how people made a living, and how debtor prison worked in nineteenth century Britain.

The Bible surpasses all books in number of copies printed and the reach of its influence. Many of us read the Bible daily and love the insights, yet few of us put forth much effort to understand the culture in which the Bible was written. This chapter will help you develop a sense of the Greco-Roman culture— of living in ancient times—with a particular focus on sex and marriage.

Adultery

The only sex mentioned on the Ten Commandment stone tablets was adultery. What does adultery mean? You know it's something about married people having sex with anyone other than their spouse...at least that's the definition today.

In Old Testament (OT) times, though, the Hebrew word for adultery (*moicheia*) was defined as a married woman having sex with any man who was not her husband. That's an asymmetric definition. The requirements are different for a woman than for a man.

A woman can't have sex with anyone except her husband. A man, on the other hand, may have sex with his slaves, prostitutes, concubines, or anyone else who is not a free and betrothed or married woman.

That's the OT definition of adultery, as well as the common understanding of it through Greco-Roman times. The stipulated penalty in the OT was death.[10]

Why were wives bound to this strict sexual fidelity when husbands were not? Inheritance. Fathers

---

[10] Leviticus 20:10, Deuteronomy 22:22; though Numbers 5: 13-30 requires the woman suspected of adultery by her jealous husband (but not caught in the act) to drink the water of bitterness (water with dust from the Temple floor). Her body is to waste away if she's guilty. I imagine most accused women hoped for the Numbers 5 penalty.

wanted to pass their assets to their true heirs. If the wife had sex with anyone else, the lineage of the heir would be questionable. Like my Dad said, "You always know who the mother is...but not so sure about the father."

To understand the sexual options open to a man in Greco-Roman times, let's hear from the fourth century BCE Greek orator Demosthenes about the three kinds of women an Athenian man can have sex with.[11]

1. **Wife**: for the birth of legitimate children
2. **Concubine**: for regular sex (may be a slave)
3. **Sexual Companion**: a prostitute trained in the sexual arts and social graces and able to accompany the man to social events, such as banquets, where wives were banned

Prostitution was legal and accepted in Greco-Roman society. The Bible has a mixed message about prostitution. Rahab the prostitute was never condemned for her job and was called one of the heroes of the faith.[12] Paul criticized prostitution—not as immoral but as polluting the male client.[13]

---

[11] Eva Cantarella, "Marriage and Divorce: Hebrew Bible: Greek World," in *The Oxford Encyclopedia of the Bible and Gender Studies*, ed. Julia M. O'Brien (New York: Oxford University Press, 2014), Volume 1, p. 490.
[12] Hebrews 11:31
[13] I Corinthians 6:15-16

We make a big mistake when we assume all cultures in all times resemble our current one. The Romans, for example, believed a woman was a vastly inferior version of a man. Women, children, slaves, effeminate men, eunuchs, etc., were all considered "non-men." All non-men lived under the authority of an elite man.

One Sex Roman Model[14]

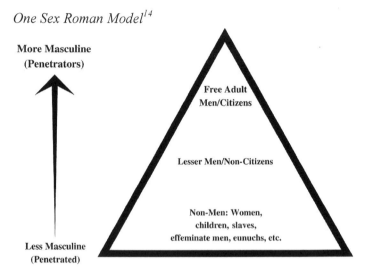

More Masculine
(Penetrators)

Free Adult
Men/Citizens

Lesser Men/Non-Citizens

Non-Men: Women,
children, slaves,
effeminate men, eunuchs, etc.

Less Masculine
(Penetrated)

When Jesus spoke about adultery, it was in this cultural context. When the Pharisees brought the woman caught in adultery to Jesus to be judged, it

---

[14] Benjamin H. Dunning, "Sexual Transgression: Roman World: New Testament," in *The Oxford Encyclopedia of the Bible and Gender Studies*, ed. Julia M. O'Brien (New York: Oxford University Press, 2014), Volume 2, p. 324.

was unsurprising that the man was not likewise accused.

After Jesus, the early church leaders struggled with the issue of adultery and forgiveness. Hemas wrote that it should be forgiven only one time, while both Tertullian and Origen thought it unforgivable. In keeping with the times, some thought that husbands could be forgiven but wives could not.[15]

Basil of Caesarea, a famous preacher and theologian alive around 350 CE, wrote that slave women sexually violated by their masters were not subject to Church discipline.[16] He also mentions no punishment for Christian masters who sexually abuse their slaves.

As you can see, the public understanding of adultery in Greco-Roman times provides a good example of the cultural context of the Bible; attitudes toward children and infants provides another.

Brutality of the Ancient World

The modern Western world took much from the cultural and government ideas of the Greek and

---

[15] Taylor G. Petrey, "Sexual Transgression: Early Church," in *The Oxford Encyclopedia of the Bible and Gender Studies*, ed. Julia M. O'Brien (New York: Oxford University Press, 2014), Volume 2, p. 337.

[16] Joy A. Schroeder, "Sexual Violence: Early Church," in *The Oxford Encyclopedia of the Bible and Gender Studies*, ed. Julia M. O'Brien (New York: Oxford University Press, 2014), Volume 2, p. 380.

Roman civilizations, yet we tend to forget how brutal many Greek and Roman values and ethics were.

Consider infanticide. It was common to kill newborns if they weren't male or if they were born with a disability or disfigurement. [17] Adding to the horrors, the method of killing was often just tossing them outside to die from exposure or to be eaten by animals. This lack of compassion for one's own children astounds the modern sensibility. Lloyd DeMause says it well:

> Infanticide during antiquity has usually been played down despite literally hundreds of clear references by ancient writers that it was an accepted, everyday occurrence. Children were thrown into rivers, flung into dung-heaps and cess trenches, "potted" in jars to starve to death, and exposed in every hill and roadside, "a prey for birds, food for wild beasts to rend" *(Euripides, Ion, 504).* [18]

In *Politics,* Aristotle wrote that children must be killed for the benefit of society:

---

[17] Katherine A. Shaner, "Family Structures: New Testament," in *The Oxford Encyclopedia of the Bible and Gender Studies*, ed. Julia M. O'Brien (New York: Oxford University Press, 2014), Volume 1, p. 219.

[18] Lloyd DeMause, *Foundations of Pyschohistory* (New York: The Institute of Physcohistory, 1982), p. 27.

> There must be a law that no imperfect or
> maimed child shall be brought up. And to
> avoid an excess in population, some children
> must be exposed. For a limit must be fixed to
> the population of the state.[19]

Four hundred years after Aristotle, Romans
continued with infanticide as normal. When Jesus
was a child, Roman citizen Hilarion wrote a letter to
his pregnant wife, Alis. It includes the following:

> Know that I am still in Alexandria. And do
> not worry if they all come back and I remain
> in Alexandria. I ask and beg of you to take
> good care of our baby son, and as soon as I
> receive payment I will send it up to you. If
> you deliver a child [before I get home], if it is
> a boy, keep it, if a girl, discard it. You have
> sent me word, "Do not forget me." How
> could I forget you? I beg you not to worry.[20]

Hilarion loved his wife but not his newborn daughter.
Infanticide was legal, considered moral, and widely
practiced.

The Bible emerged during these brutal ancient times.
Children in antiquity were an investment, not the

---

[19] Aristotle, Politics VII. 16.
[20] Cited in Naphtali Lewis, *Life in Egypt under Roman Rule* (Oxford: Clarendon, 1985), 54.

treasured beings Christianity holds them to be today. Ancient families tended to raise few children.

Family economics were tough. The Bible even provides guidelines for selling your daughter into slavery...and she can't leave the bondage after seven years as was normal for other Israelite slaves. The new master isn't allowed to sell her to a foreigner, but can keep her (presumably as a wife or concubine) or give her to his son.[21]

Let's move from that depressing topic to a quirky aside: birth defects were thought to originate from sex.[22]

- born lame = doggie style intercourse
- born mute = cunnilingus
- born deaf = conversing during sex
- born blind = man looked at vulva

The rabbi who made these observations didn't indicate any harm coming from fellatio. Big surprise, right?

Anyway, back to the brutal. No fundamental human right to life existed, and there was certainly not a

---

[21] Exodus 21:7-11

[22] Tirzah Meacham, "Male-Female Sexuality: Early Judaism," in *The Oxford Encyclopedia of the Bible and Gender Studies*, ed. Julia M. O'Brien (New York: Oxford University Press, 2014), Volume 1, p. 471.

right to a life with dignity. Consider the Roman Coliseum. Thousands of gladiators fought and died for the entertainment of the masses. Dwarfs, blind people, and people with a variety of other disabilities fought to the death in contests meant to amuse a crowd. The ancient world was harsh.

If you believe, like I do, that the Bible is completely true, then knowing the concurrent history helps increase your understanding of it. I developed a graphic at www.GreatSexChristianStyle.com that puts the Greek, Roman, and biblical times in perspective. If you want to place these times in history, have a look.

Men's and Women's Roles

Now let's get back to sex...or lack thereof. The Bible consistently states that a woman needs to be a virgin prior to and sexually faithful to her husband within marriage. A man wasn't expected to stick to either obligation. In fact, there is nothing in the Bible about whether male virginity at marriage was a rule or even desirable.

Greco-Roman culture mirrored this requirement for female virginity at marriage while including no similar obligation for males. This feels unfair from our modern perspective, but we need to understand how strong traditional gender roles were in ancient times. [23]

Men were thought to be: Women were thought to be:

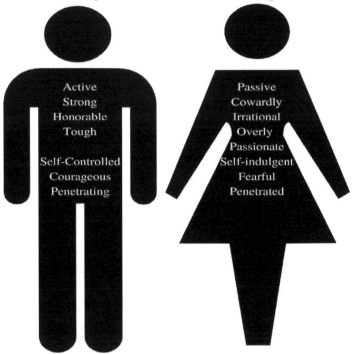

Active
Strong
Honorable
Tough

Self-Controlled
Courageous
Penetrating

Passive
Cowardly
Irrational
Overly
Passionate
Self-indulgent
Fearful
Penetrated

Since women were thought to be flighty and lacking self-control, female celibacy was assumed to be a problem. Paul addresses this issue by writing that

---

[23] Valerie Abrahamsen, "Same-Sex Relations: Early Church," in *The Oxford Encyclopedia of the Bible and Gender Studies*, ed. Julia M. O'Brien (New York: Oxford University Press, 2014), Volume 2, p. 288.

widows may remain unmarried (like Paul himself) if they have the self-control.[24] Titus writes about the same issue, concluding that young women don't have the self-control, so they should marry.[25]

The ideal man in the Greco-Roman world controlled his own passion, body, and household.[26] Women were lesser beings and were expected to be devoted to their husband and children. Women rarely learned to read and write. It was considered "unnatural" for anyone to deviate from these gender roles.

For most people in modern times, sex is a bit like a dance: there is give and take; one partner doesn't always need to lead; and there is a mutuality about it.

In Greco-Roman times, though, you were either the active penetrator or the passive receptor. To be penetrated was to be weak, to be "playing the woman," and to hold the inferior position in society.[27] The world was divided into "the penetrators" and "the penetrated."

---

[24] I Corinthians 7:7-8

[25] Titus 4:3-5

[26] Alicia D. Myers, "Religious Participation: New Testament," in *The Oxford Encyclopedia of the Bible and Gender Studies*, ed. Julia M. O'Brien (New York: Oxford University Press, 2014), Volume 2, p. 233.

[27] Eric Thurman, "Gender Transgression: Roman World," in *The Oxford Encyclopedia of the Bible and Gender Studies*, ed. Julia M. O'Brien (New York: Oxford University Press, 2014), Volume 1, p. 302.

Even more surprising to our modern thinking: that division wasn't based on gender. It had more to do with social class. A male citizen could satisfy himself sexually with his wife, concubine, slave girls, slave boys, female prostitutes, or male prostitutes. If he was the penetrator (orally, anally, or vaginally), he was within the social norms.

Sex had more to do with social position than gender in Biblical times. The elite male was "active, desiring, pursuing, initiative-taking, penetrating and getting sexual pleasure." He was the "screwer." All non-elite men and women were passive, desired, pursued, penetrated, and giving sexual pleasure." They were the "screwees." [28]

---

[28] Rosanna S. Omitowoju, "Sexual Transgression: Greek World," in *The Oxford Encyclopedia of the Bible and Gender Studies*, ed. Julia M. O'Brien (New York: Oxford University Press, 2014), Volume 2, p. 316.

Roman Sex Roles

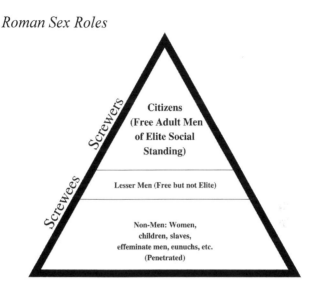

In another deviation from our modern ideas about sex, there was no requirement for consent on the part of the wife or the slaves. It was simply their duty to comply—to be the receptor. Sex by force was the right of the elite Greco-Roman male. [29] He had absolute authority over the minds and bodies of everyone in his household.

Self-Mastery Required of Men

In yet another departure from modern sensibility, the man who had too much sex, who was overly

---

[29] Marianne Blickenstaff, "Sexual Violence: New Testament," in *The Oxford Encyclopedia of the Bible and Gender Studies*, ed. Julia M. O'Brien (New York: Oxford University Press, 2014), Volume 2, p. 366.

passionate and didn't practice self-control, was criticized for being "womanly." Self-mastery was essential for the Greco-Roman elite male. As Cicero said a couple decades before Jesus was born,

> Thus everything comes down to this...that you rule yourself...not to do anything in a base, timid, ignoble, slavelike or womanish way.[30]

The assumption was that women and slaves could not control their appetites or emotions. Thus, the main character flaw of non-elite men was a lack of self-mastery over one's own body and passions, especially in terms of gluttony and lust.[31] Any intemperate behavior was considered effeminate.

Therefore, hyper-sexuality (considered macho in modern times) was considered womanish/unmanly in ancient times. Similar to gluttony, unchecked sexual activity was thought to have a debilitating effect on constitution and character.[32] For example, in Roman times it was legal and expected for a married male citizen to go to prostitutes (male or

---

[30] *Tusculan Disputations*, 2.53, 55; Epictetus 3.24.20.
[31] Eric Thurman, "Gender Transgressions: Roman World," in *The Oxford Encyclopedia of the Bible and Gender Studies*, ed. Julia M. O'Brien (New York: Oxford University Press, 2014), Volume 1, p. 299.
[32] Ibid. p 301-2.

female), but it was bad form to visit too often—to be extravagant about it.[33]

To give some context, when the Pharisees accused Jesus by calling him a glutton and drunkard, they questioned his self-mastery.[34] Thus, it was an attack on his fitness to lead.

Pederasty

Another sexual standard wildly different in ancient times is pederasty. Elite males sexually penetrating teen boys was normal in ancient Greece. This pederasty was a rite of passage for adolescent boys.

When the elite boy passed puberty at around 18 years old, he became the penetrator for the rest of his life. These relationships were common and accepted.[35]

The biggest difference in sexual standards between ancient Greece and Rome was that it was illegal to have sex with free born males in Roman times, though it was still normal for elite men to penetrate male and female slaves and prostitutes.[36]

---

[33] Benjamin H. Dunning, "Sexual Transgressions: New Testament," in *The Oxford Encyclopedia of the Bible and Gender Studies*, ed. Julia M. O'Brien (New York: Oxford University Press, 2014), Volume 2, p. 325.

[34] Matthew 11:19

[35] K. J. Dover, *Greek Homosexuality* (Cambridge, MA: Harvard University Press, 1989) p. 65.

[36] Anthony Corbeill, "Same-Sex Relations: Roman World," in *The Oxford Encyclopedia of the Bible and Gender Studies*, ed. Julia M.

The OT doesn't mention pederasty, but it doesn't seem to have been a part of Israelite culture. When Jesus spoke about the severe punishment for causing the "little ones to stumble," he seemed to be including pederasty.[37] One's hand or foot, which Jesus instructed his followers in Matthew 18:8 to cut off if it caused them to sin, was often a euphemism for the penis.[38] Jesus commanded us not to cause harm to children and seemed to view pederasty as violence—though his exact meaning isn't clearly stated.

The Household as the Basic Family Unit

Let's move on to another area that was also substantially different in ancient times: the family. Realize first that our modern concept of the nuclear family (Dad, Mom, and kids) wasn't the norm in the ancient world. In fact, there was no Roman word or phrase for that kind of family.[39]

O'Brien (New York: Oxford University Press, 2014), Volume 2, p. 271.

[37] Mark 9:42

[38] Marianne Blickenstaff, "Sexual Violence: New Testament," in *The Oxford Encyclopedia of the Bible and Gender Studies*, ed. Julia M. O'Brien (New York: Oxford University Press, 2014), Volume 2, p. 369.

[39] Helen Rhee, "Family Structures: Early Church," in *The Oxford Encyclopedia of the Bible and Gender Studies*, ed. Julia M. O'Brien (New York: Oxford University Press, 2014), Volume 1, p. 228.

The household was the basic family unit in Greco-Roman times. In Roman times it included the elite male (Paterfamilias), wife, legitimate children, slaves, extended family, adoptees, and boarders.[40] The Romans made it illegal to have more than one wife.

Roman Household

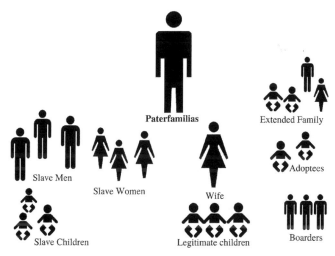

In early Greek and OT times, the head of the household could have multiple wives. Concubines were also common, as were Levirate marriages—taking the wife of one's dead brother and getting her

---

[40] Remember the movie "Oh Brother, Where Art Thou?"

pregnant so his name and inheritance could continue.[41]

The children from wives, Levirate wives, and concubines were legitimate and could participate in the inheritance. The children from slaves remained slaves and the children from prostitutes were the responsibility of the prostitute—though I imagine most of them were exposed.

Old Testament Israelite Household[42]

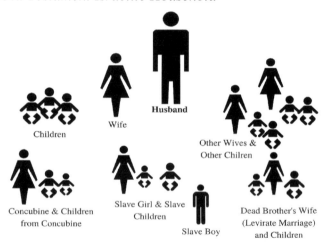

Husband

Wife

Children

Other Wives & Other Chilren

Concubine & Children from Concubine

Slave Girl & Slave Children

Slave Boy

Dead Brother's Wife (Levirate Marriage) and Children

---

[41] Genesis 38:9 tells us of Onan unwilling to impregnate his dead brother's wife per Levirate law. He and other reluctant brothers got their sandals pulled off and spit on by the widows.

[42] Jon L. Berquist, "Family Structures: Hebrew Bible," in *The Oxford Encyclopedia of the Bible and Gender Studies*, ed. Julia M. O'Brien (New York: Oxford University Press, 2014), Volume 1, p. 201.

It's important to understand that marriage/sex in OT times wasn't just between a husband and wife but between the husband and all the people sexually available to him in his household.[43] To get a sense of the times, here are the words from Demosthenes, a Greek philosopher from the 4th century BCE, on the matter:

> Mistresses we keep for pleasure, concubines for the daily attendance on our person, but wives for the procreation of legitimate children and to be faithful guardians of our household.[44]

This quote illustrates how family life morphed between ancient Greek and Israelite times. The children from the concubines of Israel became legitimate heirs, while Demosthenes indicates that those children would have been slaves. The various positions of the underlings (women and children) changed through ancient times, but the elite male remained at the top of the heap.

---

[43] Annalisa Azzoni, "Marriage and Divorce: Hebrew Bible," in *The Oxford Encyclopedia of the Bible and Gender Studies*, ed. Julia M. O'Brien (New York: Oxford University Press, 2014), Volume 1, p. 484.

[44] Demosthenes, "Apollodorus Against Neaera," *Demosthenes*, trans. by Norman W. DeWitt, Ph.D. and Norman J. DeWitt, Ph.D. (Cambridge, MA, Harvard University Press; London, William Heinemann Ltd. 1949), Section 122.

Why did elite men have that exalted position? In ancient times, battles and raids were near-daily occurrences. Young men were often killed. Famine and disease also decimated the population.

All these factors produced many young widows (with or without children). A woman had almost no opportunity to provide for herself (prostitution being a notable exception) and faced a difficult life without a husband. Polygamy in ancient times could be considered an act of compassion.

Step aside with me here to define some terms: Do you know what polygyny and polyandry mean? They are both a subset of polygamy.

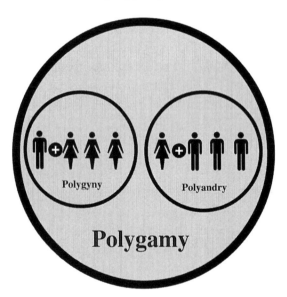

Polygyny was where one husband had multiple wives. It was common in ancient times until the Romans put an end to it. Polyandry was where one wife had multiple husbands...which doesn't seem to have existed in ancient times.[45]

To truly understand sex and marriage in the OT, we need to know that neither the OT itself nor Greek culture had any law or moral restriction against polygyny. Many Bible teachers use Genesis 2:24 ("For this reason a man will leave his father and mother and be united to his wife, and they will become one flesh") to claim that God ordained one man and one woman be married only to each other for life.

But the text says nothing about the man becoming one flesh with his second wife or the ones who followed her. Also, the Hebrew word translated as "flesh" here seems to mean kinship and doesn't have a sexual denotation. The same word is used in Genesis 29:14 when Laban said to Jacob, "Surely you are my bone and my flesh."

Since so many examples of polygyny exist in the OT, it doesn't feel honest to ignore them. In fact, the OT law states that a man can take another wife as long as

---

[45] Sarah Shectman, "Marriage and Divorce: Ancient Near East," in *The Oxford Encyclopedia of the Bible and Gender Studies,* ed. Julia M. O'Brien (New York: Oxford University Press, 2014), Volume 1, p. 481.

he provides the first wife with food, clothing, and sexual intimacy.[46]

Polygyny was common in ancient Greece and in the OT. Then, Roman law made it a serious crime to be married to more than one woman. It's significant that this rule came from the Romans and was not dictated in the Bible.[47] When Paul wrote that a deacon must be a husband of but one wife, he was following Roman law, not Hebrew law.[48]

What about ending marriages? Again, this is vastly different from modern times. The state didn't register marriages; they were a private arrangement. Divorce was easy, common, and wasn't viewed as a moral lapse, but women tended to be devastated by divorce.[49]

Here are some general standards for divorce in Biblical times.[50]

---

[46] Exodus 21:10

[47] Shulamit Valler, "Family Structures: Early Judaism," in *The Oxford Encyclopedia of the Bible and Gender Studies*, ed. Julia M. O'Brien (New York: Oxford University Press, 2014), Volume 1, p. 224.

[48] I Timothy 3:12

[49] B. Diane Lipsett, "Marriage and Divorce: Early Church," in *The Oxford Encyclopedia of the Bible and Gender Studies,* ed. Julia M. O'Brien (New York: Oxford University Press, 2014), Volume 1, p. 507.

[50] Sarah Shectman, "Marriage and Divorce: Ancient Near East," in *The Oxford Encyclopedia of the Bible and Gender Studies*, ed. Julia

1. **During the betrothal period**, the groom or bride's father could initiate divorce and there were no consequences in the separation.
2. **After marriage**, if the husband simply wanted out and no fault was found with the wife, her father (or brother) got her dowry back and kept the bride wealth.[51]
3. **If wife was found at fault** in some way, there was no financial settlement.
4. **If the wife produced children**, some minimal safeguards for the wife were provided.

When Jesus spoke against divorce, these were the standards of contemporary culture. Jesus seems to be reinforcing the sanctity of marriage and the responsibility to treat one's wife with love and kindness.[52]

We need to understand Jesus' teaching about divorce in light of his other hard teachings (do not get angry, give all possessions away, repay evil with love, etc.). He's not making rules here; he's showing us the best path and giving us the Holy Spirit.

M. O'Brien (New York: Oxford University Press, 2014), Volume 1, p. 482.

[51] The dowry was the assets the bride's family gives to the groom at marriage, while the bride wealth was the assets given by the groom's family to the bride.

[52] Matthew 19:8-12

Patriarchy

Divorce rules, polygyny, and the sexual standards of the ancient world all gave men substantial advantages over women. The term for this male-dominated hierarchical society is "Patriarchy." The word means "the rule of the father." The paterfamilias owned all the property and had legal power over his wives, children, slaves, and other household members.[53]

Did God ordain this patriarchy? The polygyny of the OT and some of Paul's statements in the NT (e.g., that women should not teach/speak in church and that they should not be elders) have led to the allegation that the Bible is a misogynistic text. But this charge ignores the cultural context.

The OT shows women as judges and leaders and contains the books of Ruth and Esther and the Song of Songs. The NT shows Jesus having support from a group made up of women and the following revolutionary listings from the book of Acts.[54]

---

[53] Deborah W. Rooke, "Patriarchy/Kyriarchy," in *The Oxford Encyclopedia of the Bible and Gender Studies,* ed. Julia M. O'Brien (New York: Oxford University Press, 2014), Volume 2, p. 1.

[54] Alicia D. Myers, "Religious Participation: New Testament," in *The Oxford Encyclopedia of the Bible and Gender Studies,* ed. Julia M. O'Brien (New York: Oxford University Press, 2014), Volume 2, p. 229.

1. **The outpouring of the Holy Spirit** went to both men and women.[55]
2. **Priscila** (whose name is always listed before her husband Aquila, which isn't normal for those times and probably shows leadership) instructed Apollos about the teachings of Jesus that went beyond John the Baptizer.[56]
3. **The four prophesying daughters of Phillip** the Evangelist are listed.[57]
4. **Tabitha** (who Peter raised from the dead) was called a disciple and was known for "always doing good and helping the poor."[58]
5. **Mary**, the mother of John Mark, hosted some of the earliest church gatherings.[59]
6. **Lydia**, a dealer in purple cloth, responds to Paul's message, and she and her entire household are baptized.[60] When Paul and Silas broke out of the prison, they went to Lydia's house to meet with other believers.[61]
7. Finally, in Thessalonica, the new believers are listed to include "**not a few prominent women**."[62]

---

[55] Acts 2:1-21
[56] Acts 18:26
[57] Acts 21:8
[58] Acts 9: 36-42
[59] Acts 12:12-17
[60] Acts 16:11-15
[61] Acts 16:40
[62] Acts 17:4

Of course, the early church was still part of a strongly patriarchal society, but when Paul writes to the Galatians that there is "no longer Jew or Greek, there is no longer slave or free, there is no longer male and female; for all of you are one in Christ Jesus," he articulates the amazing changes to come.[63]

We may wonder, "Why doesn't the NT simply condemn patriarchy?" Think about the people listening to Jesus and Paul preach. To ask those folks what they thought of patriarchy would be similar to asking fish what they think of water. There simply wasn't a conceivable alternative.

Yet, we all get to interpret the Bible in our own way; that is part of the incredible freedom God gives us. My study of the Bible and related ancient texts convinces me that the Bible was written in patriarchal times but points us toward a time when patriarchy is no more.

Sadly, that journey has taken a couple thousand years and is still only partially completed. I'm saddened when men use the writings of Paul, who I find remarkably egalitarian, as a hammer to force women into positions of subservience and tell them that they are less than equal partners. That behavior seems to go against our goal to become more and more Christ-like.

---

[63] Galatians 3:28

Beyond Patriarchy

The New Testament provides, as its name suggests, *new* teaching that will eventually move the world beyond patriarchy. The NT takes us beyond rule-based living. We are encouraged to rely on the leading of the Holy Spirit, and that changes everything. Let's look at some of those teachings that relate to sex and marriage.

Paul recommends lots of sex in marriage. He says the Christian husband and wife will be best protected from sexual sins with others if they regularly service each other.[64] Paul further veers from the patriarchy of the day to state that women have sexual needs that must also be met. He even mentions that women may take the lead in the marriage to meet those needs.[65]

Of course, Paul couches these directives with his belief that people would be better off if they focused fully on Jesus, didn't marry, and ignored sex. Yet, he acknowledges that such an idea simply isn't realistic for most people. If it isn't for you, then you should marry and have enough sex to keep yourself and your partner satisfied.[66]

---

[64] I Corinthians 7:2-5

[65] Kathy L. Gaca, "Male-Female Sexuality: Early Church," in *The Oxford Encyclopedia of the Bible and Gender Studies,* ed. Julia M. O'Brien (New York: Oxford University Press, 2014), Volume 1, p. 474.

[66] I Corinthians 7: 1-10

In a fascinating twist, the early church in 400 to 500 CE moved away from Paul's sex-positive teaching. Many church leaders wrote that sex should be for procreation only.[67] In fact, celibacy within marriage became the ideal. Sex was to be performed without desire (don't try this at home) and only for the purpose of procreation.[68]

Why the shift? For the first few hundred years, the early Church grew and struggled to define itself. After Constantine took power in the early 300s, he not only made Christianity legal but made it the official religion. He helped develop the Nicene Creed, which preceded the Apostle's Creed. With a Christian Roman emperor, the early believers went from being considered criminals to taking hold of some power.

Of course, it's no fun having power if you can't make rules for other people. To contrast itself against the libertine Greek and Roman cultures, sex and marriage rules became more stringent.

---

[67] Kathy L. Gaca, "Male-Female Sexuality: Early Church," in *The Oxford Encyclopedia of the Bible and Gender Studies,* ed. Julia M. O'Brien (New York: Oxford University Press, 2014), Volume 1, p. 475.

[68] Taylor G. Petrey, "Sexual Transgression: Early Church," in *The Oxford Encyclopedia of the Bible and Gender Studies,* ed. Julia M. O'Brien (New York: Oxford University Press, 2014), Volume 2, p. 338.

The early church pondered celibate marriages, marriage to non-Christians, and second marriages. By the 400s, Christians truly broke from the Greco-Roman world by banning forced prostitution and same sex intercourse.[69] Remember, in this time, it was common for a man to have sex with a prostitute. It was legal and not considered a moral transgression.

Paul told believers not to engage with prostitutes right after telling them not to sue.[70] He wasn't setting up new rules (that just wasn't Paul); he was encouraging believers to live up to a higher standard. Paul condemned sex with prostitutes because it polluted the body of Christ, not the marriage bed.[71]

I don't want to minimize Paul's teaching, though. He clearly told us to flee from sexual immorality and to honor God with our bodies.

The early Christians, and every group thereafter, has been trying to figure out what really constitutes "sexual immorality." Do we go with the teaching that God created the body above the navel, while Satan created the bottom half ?[72] Then we must choose celibacy. Perhaps we conclude that celibacy is good for some, but not for us?

---

[69] Ibid.
[70] I Corinthians 6:16
[71] I Corinthians 6:12-20
[72] Basil of Ancyra (*de Virginitate*, 7, Migne, *P.G.*, XXX, 684 A)

It's important for us to understand that Jesus didn't directly challenge the patriarchy of his time. He didn't call for an immediate social upheaval; he didn't call for the end of slavery or prostitution or for infants to stop being exposed. Rather, he planted the seeds for the future destruction of the patriarchal system.

For example, when the Pharisees asked Jesus a tempting question about divorce, he responds by outlining God's perfect plan for marriage.[73] Later in that chapter, Jesus outlines God's perfect plan for giving—telling the rich young ruler to sell all his possessions and give the money to the poor.[74] In neither case was Jesus making new laws for us to live by.

Many rules emerged in the first few hundred years of the early church. Some of the rules the early church instituted make perfect sense in our modern context. Stopping the practice of exposing infants right after birth is certainly a more humane way of doing things.[75] Rules made divorce more difficult to obtain and forced the husband to answer to the church as to why he demanded a divorce, which put the wife in a more protected position.

---

[73] Matthew 19:3
[74] Matthew 19:16-30
[75] B. Diane Lipsett, "Marriage and Divorce: Early Church," in *The Oxford Encyclopedia of the Bible and Gender Studies,* ed. Julia M. O'Brien (New York: Oxford University Press, 2014), Volume 1, p. 508.

Of course, all institutions with power seem to overplay their hands, and the early church certainly did...as does the modern church. Tertullian wrote that marriage was not forbidden, but that didn't make it good. He pushed for celibacy within marriage. He also called marriage after divorce a "sexual crime."[76] This anti-sex attitude of the early church—which is nowhere to be found in Christ's or Paul's teachings—has stayed in the church for centuries.

Christians have constantly changed their moral standards and rules throughout history. The base of Christian teaching that has never changed is grace, forgiveness, and love. We've gone wrong in many ways with our moral standards and rules, but we've never gone wrong with grace, forgiveness and love. We live best when we focus on the two commandments from Jesus: Honor God and love others.

---

[76] Taylor G. Petrey, "Sexual Transgression: Early Church," in *The Oxford Encyclopedia of the Bible and Gender Studies,* ed. Julia M. O'Brien (New York: Oxford University Press, 2014), Volume 2, p. 337.

Chapter 3

Oral Sex: Let's Talk About It

Oral sex rocks. Almost anyone can bring about amazing orgasms through oral sex—even a Bozo like me who has minimal sense of rhythm and whose mind wanders most of the time. The tongue works as the perfect sex tool. It's sensitive and just a quick swallow away from the wonderful sex lubricant that is saliva. The face and brain being in such close proximity makes it even better. I love oral sex.

So why do many Christian couples abstain from oral sex? Some think it's sinful, though there doesn't seem to be any biblical backing for that idea. In fact, the Song of Solomon contains passages that seem to describe a woman performing oral sex on a man:

> *Like an apple tree among the trees of the forest is my lover among the young men. I delight to sit in his shade, and his fruit is sweet to my taste.*[77]

---

[77] Song of Songs 2:3

In a similar way, the Bride speaks of a man performing oral sex on a woman:

Awake, north wind, and come, south wind! Blow on my garden, that its fragrance may spread abroad. Let my lover come into his garden and taste its choice fruits. [78]

You could argue that the author isn't describing oral sex, but it seems to be the most obvious reading. As with most Bible interpretation, you get to decide.

Is Oral Sex for You?

I have no idea if you and your spouse should be going down on each other. If you struggle with the concept, go to the Lord in prayer and the Holy Spirit will give you guidance.

Remember, if you're very interested and your partner is very opposed, please don't try to force your will. The Bible tells us many times to be kind and to try not to force our will on others. So please don't use the above verses as a hammer to get your way. Hopefully your sex life, like the rest of your life, involves a constant striving to control your own selfishness and laziness while loving your spouse.

In our relationships with others, especially our spouse, we should be looking to I Corinthians 13 as

---

[78] Song of Songs 4:16

our behavior guide. Let's look at it now and see how we fair:

Love is patient, love is kind. It does not envy, it does not boast, it is not proud. It is not rude, it is not self-seeking, it is not easily angered, it keeps no record of wrongs. Love does not delight in evil but rejoices with the truth. It always protects, always trusts, always hopes, always perseveres.

Whether you're talking about oral sex or deciding where to have supper, this self-sacrificing love should be your model. When you both try it, even in our vastly imperfect humanness, the results amaze.

What if one of you thinks that oral sex is simply disgusting? As challenging as these things are to discuss, it's worth the effort. You may conclude that it's not for you and your marriage. That's fine. We all get to decide how to live our weird, short little lives. Just don't default to "No" on everything that takes you out of your comfort zone. Too many Christians tiptoe through life to get to death safely.

So what other objections to oral sex, besides "it's sinful" or "I just don't want to," are there? Cleanliness tends to be another big one. Lots of women have the idea that they are dirty or smelly down there (it seems few men have that concern for themselves).

In reality, genitals of a healthy person that have been recently washed tend to be cleaner than our mouths.

Men, assure your partner that God made the female genitals as one of the most self-cleaning and self-maintaining areas on her body. Generally, the slight odor from clean female genitals are a turn-on for the male. Men are designed to like that musky smell.

If it's a new act for you, take a bath or shower together first. The act of washing each other builds intimacy and trust and helps remove the smell concern. As with all sexual techniques, don't just start in like you're going to work. Remember romance, preparation, relaxation, and fun.

Cunnilingus

What do you see between a woman's legs? Most folks would say the vagina. Most folks would be wrong, which shouldn't surprise us. The "vulva" is the correct name for a woman's external genital area.

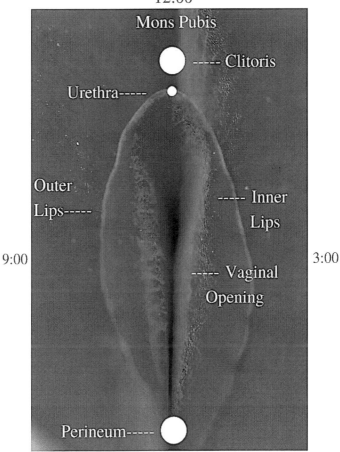

Anus as depicted by Kurt Vonnegut, Jr.

The vulva includes:

1. **Mons Pubis or "Pubic Mound"** is the rounded mass of fatty tissue atop the pubic bone and covered with pubic hair. The mons pubis is at the top of the vulva at the 12:00 position.

2. **Perineum or the "Taint"** is the small, smooth, hairless area at the bottom of the vulva, located between the anus and the vagina opening. Located at the 6:00 position.

3. **Outer lips or "Labia Majora"** are longitudinal skin folds that run from the mons pubis to the perineum. The outer lips are similar to the male scrotum and tend to have pubic hair. Located at the 3:00 and 9:00 positions.

4. **Inner lips or "Labia Minora"** are flaps of skin, generally hairless, located inside the outer lips. The inner lips vary widely in size, color, and shape from woman to woman. The inner lips are similar to the male penile skin. Located at the 3:00 and 9:00 positions.

5. **Clitoral Hood** is at the top of the inner lips and is similar to the foreskin of an uncircumcised penis. This small fold of skin protects or folds over the clitoris.

6. **Clitoris** (pronounced CLIT-or-is or cli-Tor-is) is often quite small until stimulated, but then it may grow to ½ to 1" long. The tip or glans is extremely sensitive, more so than the head of a penis. The shaft is also sensitive.

7. **Urethral opening** is located between the clitoris and the vagina, but you won't find it unless you see a urine stream coming out of it. There is no real reason to find it; it is just good to know it's there.

8. **Vagina opening**: Generally, the outer and inner lips need to be spread apart to see the vagina opening. It is located at the center of the clock.

If you want to pleasure a woman, study all the parts of the vulva. Study it like you were planning to take a test. Then, experiment with stroking, licking, kissing, nibbling or blowing and find what she likes and what she doesn't. One word of caution: never blow into the vaginal opening, you could introduce dangerous air bubbles into the blood.

Some specific directions for a man to perform oral sex on a woman (AKA cunnilingus): First, what not to do. Don't go in there lapping like a dog eating peanut butter. Remember the amazing sensitivity of the clitoris. Also, remember this isn't a race to an orgasm. The goal is to give pleasure and enjoy doing it. Sometimes orgasms will follow from that, but don't make that the goal. Don't make the orgasm the measure of success.

Now that you've got the lay of the land, let's cover some emotional issues surrounding the area. Many women struggle with how their vulvas look; they often think their vulva looks wrong, perhaps because it doesn't look like what they've seen in magazines or videos. Vulvas can look incredibly different, and you should praise your partner's vulva. Also take the opportunity to compliment the sweet smell. Cunnilingus uses all five senses. Learn to enjoy each of those senses and to let your wife know the specifics of what you're enjoying sensually.

Now let's dive into more detailed advice. Hopefully you've taken some time to explore and pleasure other parts of her body. Facing the situation, as it were, don't just to stick out your tongue and say, "Ahhhh." Consider some technique training.

Put your hand in front of your face and imagine it's a vulva (you now know the parts). Lick your palm imagining the vulva. Feel silly? Great. It's good for the soul to feel a little silly sometimes.

So what's the first thing you notice when you lick your palm? You probably wonder where to start and how to lick. Then, after you start licking you'll notice how quickly your tongue gets dry. A dry tongue produces too much friction. Remember to keep dipping it back in your mouth for more saliva. Think "fountain pen."

Now try to vary the hardness of your tongue. You can use a broad, relaxed tongue for a gentle stroke or a more pointed, tensed tongue for a hard stroke. If this all sounds like French to you, well, it is.

Then try various stroke types:
1. **Up only** (not licking on the down stroke)
2. **Down only** (not licking on the up stroke)
3. **Up and down** (licking on both strokes)
4. **Side to side** (licking on both strokes)
5. **Circular**
6. **Geometric shapes**
7. **Alphabet letter shapes**

My favorite multi-tasking event for my Type A personality came from doing alphabet letter shapes. I was planning a trip to Russia and learning to speak some basic Russian. This study involved learning the Cyrillic alphabet, which is similar to the English alphabet but has a bunch of different letters. So I'd trace those letters with my tongue on my lover's clitoris, giving pleasure while learning Russian. And yes, I know I'm a weirdo.

The beauty of tracing letters, though, is the randomness of the motion. Due to the amazing sensitivity of the clitoris, the random motion often works well in the early stages of oral sex. Of course, every woman experiences it differently, as does the same woman in a different mood. The key is to try, talk, laugh, and try some more. Encourage her to tell you or indicate in another way what she likes.

Since the vulva has amazing sensitivity, use other methods to activate its nerve endings. Playing with hot and cold can be fun. Munch on some ice chips to make your tongue cold, or drink a nice hot beverage to create some steam down there. These can also feel good on nipples, neck, belly, or other areas of the body. Try varying the hot and cold to really mix it up.

Warming lubes also create a pleasant heat. Just remember to use caution on sensitive areas. "Remember, be careful down there."[79]

You can also try menthol to stimulate the genitals. Use mouthwash prior to your next trip south, or try one of those intense mint lozenges. You can go as far as pressing the mint against various parts of the vulva (this may be too intense, so ask how it feels). Just having mint flavored saliva can create a tingling sensation.

---

[79] Paraphrase from Sgt. Phil Esterhaus of the Hill Street Blues.

Suction can also be a pleasant process. The inner thighs, outer lips, inner lips and clitoris all can be Hoovered with pleasant results. Again, check to make sure that the pressure isn't too much and vary the location and pressure often. Stay below the "Hickey Level" of suction. You aren't in high school any more. Unless you are…then feel free to hickey at will.

Here are some other useful tips:
1. **Don't assume** any correlation between the way you like your penis sucked and the way your lover will like her vulva stimulated.
2. **Scratchy Beard Face** is a no-no down there.
3. **Porn videos show nothing useful** about oral sex, it's a stupid show based on camera angles
4. **Ask your partner** what she likes and pay attention to how she moves. Make your oral sex practice a continuous learning experience.

Again, don't make sex all about the orgasm. Focus on love and pleasure and fun. And when the orgasm follows from that love, pleasure, and fun, it is wonderful. Let's discuss that little bit of wonderful.

When you perform oral sex and start feeling more lubrication and notice her moving and perhaps moaning, she is probably getting close to an orgasm.

If you were masturbating, you would grip harder and go faster. Don't do that.

Most women approaching orgasm want you to keep doing exactly what you are doing. Don't go faster, don't go slower, don't start discussing French poetry. Just keep doing what you are doing. Even as she orgasms, it generally feels best for you to just continue on with more of the same until it's over.

Here are a few additional tips from the weirdly and wonderfully encyclopedic book *Guide to Getting it On*.[80]

1. **Don't start right in on the clitoris**. Start slowly, working around the outer area of the vulva and thighs. Take your time.
2. **Try pillows** under her butt for optimum placement.
3. **Try to lick through her panties** sometimes. This can be a gentle way to start. Eventually, pull the fabric aside for better access.
4. **Oral sex on a woman who is standing** doesn't work well.
5. **Tongue and Vibrator**: When your spouse is highly aroused, consider putting your tongue right under her clitoris and a small vibrator below your tongue.
6. **Try some fruit**, like banana or mango, down there. Use caution, though, with fruit, honey,

---

[80] Paul Joannides, *Guide to Getting It On: A Book About the Wonders of Sex* (Oregon: Goofy Foot Press, 2014), 277.

or chocolate syrup because the sugars can cause yeast infections.

7. **Towel**: Consider keeping a towel underneath for fluid control and a washcloth nearby for cleanup.

8. **Counting**: Here's an advanced move for you over-achievers: Bring your spouse to the edge of orgasm, then kiss around the edges of the vulva for a count of 50. Go back to the clitoris and get to the edge of orgasm, then do something else for a count of 25. Do it again for a count of 10, then for a few seconds, and then finish things off.

Finally, you may want to think of your wife's vulva (or her entire body) as a map. Explore and learn her areas of high and low sensitivity. Pay attention to what stimulates her and what annoys her. Don't take it too personally if sometimes your existence seems to be what annoys her most. Keep humbly trying to love her and make her feel good.

Fellatio

Now let's consider my favorite topic: fellatio, a woman performing oral sex on a man. It's a fairly straight forward deal. Unlike all the complexities of the vulva, the penis just sticks out there like a popsicle...or a banana.

The first important item is for the male genital area to be clean. The heat and sweaty moisture down there can cause bacteria growth. No one wants that. Start by getting clean.

As you contemplate fellatio, consider how it's going to end. There are really only two options. Either the fellatio is a bit of foreplay that then moves on to some other sexual shenanigans or it ends with ejaculation. If it's the latter, women have three options:

1. Take the ejaculate in your mouth and then spit it out.
2. Take the ejaculate in your mouth and swallow it.
3. Let the ejaculate fly into the air.

So the options are spit, swallow, or fly. Which is the right way to go? It's up to you.

Don't be pressured into doing something you really don't like. On the other hand, I can tell you that orgasming into a mouth feels wonderful. But since the whole process feels pretty wonderful, don't feel it has to end a certain way in order to be acceptable. Emily Post has no rules for fellatio.

Let's talk quickly about gag prevention. Remember the 1970s porn movie *Deep Throat*? Everyone has heard of it, but few people have seen it. The premise was that a woman needs to take the whole (and weirdly huge) penis in the mouth to do it right. That's a silly idea. If your husband pushes this idea, buy him a cucumber about his size and ask him to show you how it's done. Of course if he likes that, you may have another problem.

Back to gag prevention. Most men will have a natural tendency just before and during orgasm to want to thrust forward and go deeper. Hence, the tendency to gag. You can talk about this, though your mouth may be full at the time, and many folks are uncomfortable talking about these kinds of things. So while I encourage you to speak up, I understand many women won't.

If you don't want to talk about it, try placing your fist around the bottom of the penis, like you were grabbing onto a pole. With your fist in this position, you create a stop on the penis that only lets the exposed part above your thumb into your mouth. If your spouse has been especially gifted, you may need to grab it with both hands like a baseball bat.

Now let's get down to what really great fellatio might include.

1. **Saliva:** The extra lubricant works better for everyone. Drool running down a penis makes for better hand pumping at the lower end of the shaft. You can put a towel under him if you don't want a spit spot on the sheets when you're done. For me, avoiding the spot is good post coital exercise.

2. **Soft or Hard, it's all good:** Don't worry if your man isn't hard. It's going to feel great either way. Let him just relax and feel no pressure to perform.

3. **Frenulum, the secret spot:** The most sensitive spot on a penis is on the bottom, just below the head. It's called the frenulum. If you don't want his penis in your mouth, you can lick and suck this area while using both hands on his penis and testicles. If he's on his back and you are laying off to the side, you will be in position to do this. Remember to use lots of saliva on the frenulum and kiss like you're back in high school.

4. **Teeth:** I remember snorkeling in the Caribbean and seeing a barracuda with its big teeth. Ladies, listen: when your teeth touch a penis during fellatio, the barracuda is likely the image that comes to his mind. Be careful.

As always, you may want to just ask. Some men like the feeling of choppers chomping.

5. **Sealing the seam:** On the underside of the penis, there is a seam that runs from the head to the scrotum (I'm sure, I just checked). Try giving a long wet lick from the scrotum, along the seam, and all the way to the head— like licking an envelope.

6. **Suck and pump:** Take the penis head in your mouth, bob up and down, and add some pleasant variety by grabbing the lower part of the penis shaft with your hand and pumping in time with your mouth. Again, let some saliva roll down the shaft for better lubrication.

7. **Perineum tickle:** The perineum (also called the taint) is the highly sensitive area between the scrotum and the anus. Licking or lightly touching this area adds wonderful variety in fellatio.

8. **Hot, cold, and menthol:** Just like different temperatures can create wonderful sensations during oral sex on a woman, great feelings can follow from a mouthful of ice chips, hot tea, or a strong mint.

9. **All hands on deck:** You may want to use your hands as well as your mouth to up the eroticism. Rubbing his nipples, tickling his scrotum, pulling his butt towards you, or any of dozens of other antics can make him feel great.

10. **Your two new best friends:** Pay particular attention to the testicles. Kissing them or taking one into your mouth and gently sucking it will be a big turn-on…unless, of course, it's not. As always, talk about it.

11. **Multi-tasking Masturbation:** If you like to multi-task, you may want to masturbate as you're performing fellatio. It will certainly turn him on all the more. Using a mirror so he can watch you masturbate also adds to the experience.

12. **Sound Vibrations:** Moaning or any kind of enthusiastic sex noises while performing fellatio adds a wonderful vibration on the penis. Plus, the man will be much more excited knowing you are enjoying yourself down there. The less it seems a chore for you, the better it will be for both of you.

All the above techniques can be wonderful and appreciated. But remember, this ends in one of two ways. Either you move on to other intimacies (with a very appreciative partner who should now be treating you like a queen) or go all the way to ejaculation.

If you opt for ejaculation, you can learn to know when that train is about to leave the station. The penis will swell more and start to throb. He may moan and move more. A bit of pre-ejaculate often escapes as well. When you recognize the time approaching, you get to decide how you want to handle this momentous occasion. You have the spit, swallow, or fly decision.

Anything you try will probably be appreciated. Enthusiasm trumps technique, though great technique is a wonderful thing. If you're only doing it because you feel you have to, it won't be nearly as good for him as it will be if you are into it. Have fun pleasing each other. And remember oral sex for a last-minute gift idea.

One final note: Don't feel pressured into anything, and don't pressure your partner into anything. It all works best when it comes from a practice of deep mutual love and submission. And a quick note to husbands: be careful thrusting into her mouth or controlling her head with your hand. What feels natural to you may feel miserable for her. Learn how to receive without being selfish. You'll both enjoy oral sex a lot more when it's about mutual and equal give and take.

Chapter 4
God Talks Sex

King Solomon wrote over 1,000 songs. The title of his biblical book "The Song of Songs" means the song is Solomon's best song. Some Jewish scholars postulate the book describes God's love for Israel. Some Christian scholars see the relationship between Christ and the Church in the song verses. I see sex, as do many other commentators. That's the obvious reading, so let's go with it and take it as God telling us about sex.

Thoughts on "The Song of Songs"

Below are the lines that inspire me. I include my weird commentary on each of those verses. Read the snippets below and decide for yourself if God gave us sex as a wonderful gift:

1:2 She says: *Let him kiss me with the kisses of his mouth—for your love is more delightful than wine.* Wine is delightful, but sex is even more delightful.

1:3 She says: *Take me away with you—let us hurry!* The urgency of passion; we've all been there.

1:6 She says: *Do not stare at me because I am dark, because I am darkened by the sun.* She has a charming shyness, perhaps about her lover seeing her naked tan lines.

1:8 He says: *If you do not know, most beautiful of women.* Flattery will get him everywhere.

1:9 He says: *I liken you, my darling, to a mare harnessed to one of the chariots of Pharaoh.* Now that's a compliment not often heard these days...I suppose it could be flattering...

1:12 She says: *While the king was at his table, my perfume spread its fragrance.* This may mean she became aroused, the perfume being a euphemism for natural sexual fluids and their musky odor.

1:13 She says: *My lover is to me a sachet of myrrh resting between my breasts.* She has him where she wants him and he smells great.

1:15 He says: *How beautiful you are, my darling! Oh, how beautiful! Your eyes are doves.* Again with the flattery.

1:16 She says: *How handsome you are, my lover! Oh, how charming! And our bed is verdant.* When I checked my Funk and Wagnall, I found that either they are laying in the grass or on green sheets.

1:17 He says: *The beams of our house are cedars; our rafters are firs.* Sure seems to imply that he's talking about his erections, and there's no mention of a blue pill.

2:2 He says: *Like a lily among thorns is my darling among the maidens.* She's prettier than all other girls. Flattery again, but I bet he believes it.

2:3 She says: *Like an apple tree among the trees of the forest is my lover among the young men. I delight to sit in his shade, and his fruit is sweet to my taste.* She loves to pleasure him with fellatio.

2:4 She says: *He has taken me to the banquet hall, and his banner over me is love.* Two beautiful analogies for passion.

2.5 She says: *Strengthen me with raisins, refresh me with apples, for I am faint with love.* Long lovemaking sessions need carb-refuel breaks.

2:7 She says: *Do not arouse or awaken love until it so desires.* Don't just scratch the itch; make love making wonderful.

2:8-9 She says: *Listen! My lover! Look! Here he comes, leaping across the mountains, bounding over the hills. My lover is like a gazelle or a young stag.* She's visually attracted to him. She feels his approach.

2:13 She says: *The fig tree forms its early fruit; the blossoming vines spread their fragrance. Arise, come, my darling; my beautiful one, come with me.* The early fruit of the fig tree seems to be a euphemism for his erection and the blossoming vines spreading their fragrance seems to be a euphemism for her legs spreading and her building arousal.

2:14 He says: *My dove in the clefts of the rock, in the hiding places on the mountainside, show me your face, let me hear your voice; for your voice is sweet, and your face is lovely.* He's looking for her, desiring her, and trying to connect with her.

2:15 He says: *Catch for us the foxes, the little foxes that ruin the vineyards, our vineyards that are in bloom.* Perhaps the foxes are the little cares and annoyances that distract from focused lovemaking.

2:16 She says: *My lover is mine and I am his; he browses among the lilies.* He pleasures her with cunnilingus.

2:17 She says: *Until the day breaks and the shadows flee, turn, my lover, and be like a gazelle or like a young stag on the rugged hills.* They make love outside throughout the night. Then she tells him to go on his way. I'm not sure of their marital status here, but this doesn't seem like married people sex.

4:1 He says: *How beautiful you are, my darling! Oh, how beautiful! Your eyes behind your veil are doves. Your hair is like a flock of goats descending from Mount Gilead.* Beautiful language. When our son-in-law first met our daughter on a blind date, they sat down in a restaurant and she removed her winter hat. Her curls tumbled down to her shoulders. He gasped in involuntary awe. He had her at the gasp. The same kind of thing seems to be happening here.

4:3 He says: *Your lips are like a scarlet ribbon; your mouth is lovely. Your temples behind your veil are like the halves of a pomegranate.* Lips, teeth, and mouth are such integral parts of lovemaking. This verse, along with verses 4 and 5, remind me of Al Pacino in the movie *Scent of a Woman*, where he describes, in coarser language, the feminine attractions.

4:7 He says: *All beautiful you are, my darling; there is no flaw in you.* We can all feel that way about our partner in a special moment, can't we?

4:9-15 He says: *You have stolen my heart, my sister, my bride; you have stolen my heart with one glance of your eyes, with one jewel of your necklace.*
How delightful is your love, my sister, my bride! How much more pleasing is your love than wine, and the fragrance of your perfume than any spice!
Your lips drop sweetness as the honeycomb, my bride; milk and honey are under your tongue. The fragrance of your garments is like that of Lebanon.
You are a garden locked up, my sister, my bride; you are a spring enclosed, a sealed fountain.
Your plants are an orchard of pomegranates with choice fruits, with henna and nard,
nard and saffron, calamus and cinnamon, with every kind of incense tree, with myrrh and aloes and all the finest spices.
You are a garden fountain, a well of flowing water streaming down from Lebanon.
He's full of love and analogies for great sex. He's a happy guy.

4:16 She says: *Awake, north wind, and come, south wind! Blow on my garden, that its fragrance may spread abroad. Let my lover come into his garden and taste its choice fruits.* She requests cunnilingus with a "gentle blowing," a light touch.

5:4 She says: *My lover thrust his hand through the latch opening; my heart began to pound for him.* The word translated "latch opening" is also the word for hole...you get it.

5:10 She says: *My lover is radiant and ruddy, outstanding among ten thousand.* She values him.

5:11 She says: *His head is purest gold; his hair is wavy and black as a raven.* He has great hair.

5:12 She says: *His eyes are like doves by the water streams, washed in milk, mounted like jewels.* He has great eyes.

5:13 She says: *His cheeks are like beds of spice yielding perfume. His lips are like lilies dripping with myrrh.* He has a great face.

5:14-15 She says: *His arms are rods of gold set with chrysolite. His body is like polished ivory decorated with sapphires. His legs are pillars of marble set on bases of pure gold. His appearance is like Lebanon, choice as its cedars.* He has a great physique and an erect penis.

5:16 She says: *His mouth is sweetness itself; he is altogether lovely. This is my lover, this my friend, O daughters of Jerusalem.* His kisses are altogether lovely. He's her lover and friend, which is a beautiful gift from God.

6:2-3 She says: *My lover has gone down to his garden, to the beds of spices, to browse in the gardens and to gather lilies. I am my lover's and my lover is mine; he browses among the lilies.* He explores the wonders of her vulva.

6:4 He says: *You are beautiful, my darling, as Tirzah, lovely as Jerusalem, majestic as troops with banners.* Here's another odd compliment: "As lovely as troops with banners." On the other hand, he's the guy with a 1,000 wives and concubines, so maybe he knows a few things I don't.

6:5 He says: *Turn your eyes from me; they overwhelm me. Your hair is like a flock of goats descending from Gilead.* Asking her to avert her eyes because she overwhelms him is certainly charming, as is the complement to her hair.

6:6 He says: *Your teeth are like a flock of sheep coming up from the washing. Each has its twin, not one of them is alone.* All teeth are present and accounted for; no hillbilly smile here.

7:1 He says: *How beautiful your sandaled feet, O prince's daughter! Your graceful legs are like jewels, the work of a craftsman's hands.* She has great legs.

7:2 He says: *Your navel is a rounded goblet that never lacks blended wine. Your waist is a mound of wheat encircled by lilies.* I believe this is the first mention in history of belly button shots, though the symbol for the navel may be in reference instead to the vulva.

7:3 He says: *Your breasts are like two fawns, twins of a gazelle.* When I walk through the woods and see two white tailed deer fawns, I am filled with joy. Seeing my wife's breasts still does that for me.

7:5 He says: *Your head crowns you like Mount Carmel. Your hair is like royal tapestry; the king is held captive by its tresses.* Funny to think of the King held captive by the beautiful hair of a peasant girl, but that's the stuff all Disney princess stories are made of.

7:6 He says: *How beautiful you are and how pleasing, O love, with your delights!* Think about the delights of love; it's a list of activities that can just keep growing.

7:7 He says: *Your stature is like that of the palm, and your breasts like clusters of fruit.* She has great posture and breasts unaffected by gravity.

7:8 He says: *I said, "I will climb the palm tree; I will take hold of its fruit." May your breasts be like the clusters of the vine, the fragrance of your breath like apples.* Wonderfully graphic sex talk. He's ready to get busy.

7:9 She says: *And your mouth like the best wine. May the wine go straight to my lover, flowing gently over lips and teeth.* Wine is an aphrodisiac.

7:10 She says: *I belong to my lover, and his desire is for me.* Ah, the mutual submission of great lovemaking.

7:12-13 She says: *Let us go early to the vineyards to see if the vines have budded, if their blossoms have opened, and if the pomegranates are in bloom—there I will give you my love. The mandrakes send out their fragrance, and at our door is every delicacy, both new and old, that I have stored up for you, my lover.* A good reminder to use fragrances in love making. Each of our five senses can be pleasured. The door refers to an opening (vagina).

8:10 She says: *I am a wall, and my breasts are like towers. Thus I have become in his eyes like one bringing contentment.* Those towering breasts seemed to make him happy. One aspect of the joy of sex is that it has the potential to make both husband and wife feel content.

8:14 She says: *Come away, my lover, and be like a gazelle or like a young stag on the spice-laden mountains.* She really likes sex.

Now that you've read through these verses and musings, think more about the Song of Songs. It is clearly a love story. It is sometimes the love story between a rural girl and her shepherd lover and other times between peasant girl at court and a handsome king. Neither the woman nor the man is named, but Solomon is mentioned. This could be a literary technique called "King fiction," where challenging texts are made more acceptable since the leading character is a king. In the ancient world, leaders got to play by different rules.[81] Glad that doesn't still happen.[82]

The Song of Songs teaches about passion, desire, and sex. While many folks find sex shameful, embarrassing, and ungodly, God doesn't seem to share that opinion.

What conclusions do I draw, then, from the above? God gave us sex to enjoy, to celebrate, to revere. He inspired the Song of Songs to give us some directions in the act of lovemaking. I don't know about you, but I'm trained to follow orders.

---

[81] Carole R. Fontaine, "Imagery, Gendered: Wisdom Literature," in *The Oxford Encyclopedia of the Bible and Gender Studies,* ed. Julia M. O'Brien (New York: Oxford University Press, 2014), Volume 1, p. 365.
[82] By the way, Solomon had 300 wives and 700 concubines (I Kings 11:3). Commentators that try to make the book about the sanctity of traditional marriage have to ignore that.

Chapter 5

Aphrodisiacs:
Who-ahhh!

Through history, people yearned for aphrodisiacs. Like medieval knights searching for the Holy Grail, people wanted the secret ingredient that makes sex better. Aphrodisiac means "arousing or intensifying sexual desire," but we'll use a broader definition that includes:

1. the lowering of sexual inhibitions
2. the intensifying of sexual desire
3. the increase of sexual pleasure

The effectiveness of aphrodisiacs has always been murky. In Macbeth, Shakespeare wrote that alcohol "provokes the desire, but it takes away the performance."

Viagra, on the other hand, has no direct effect on sexual desire. But it gives an erection that, according to the ads, can last for hours. So Viagra is a performance item (or perhaps a form of torture).

Confused? Good. Let's start at the beginning. Desire precedes performance. So what drives desire?

Fruits of the Spirit

God gave us a clue for making ourselves desirable to him and to one another in Galatians 5:22. The Fruits of the Spirit are love, joy, peace, patience, kindness, goodness, faithfulness, gentleness, and self-control. As we strive each day to live into these attributes, we make ourselves attractive to our spouses. We create desire and intimacy.

I developed an expansion of the Fruits of the Spirit that I repeat almost every day. It helps me move in the direction of living the Fruits. I encourage you to make this part of your daily prayer time:

Love

Let me judicially give and judicially withhold, to know that love is action, and to act. Let me care about others more than myself.

Joy

Help me to have the happiness that comes from knowing I am doing Your will on Earth. Give me lightness that flows out of You that I may feel and others may see. Help me not be depressed or dreary.

Peace

Give me that sense of calm that comes from knowing how much You love me and that nothing happens apart from You in this universe. Give me the peace that passes understanding.

Patience

Allow me to live in a way that acknowledges Your timing, to know that I can't always have what I want when I want it, and to be mature enough to accept Your will.

Kindness

Show me the heart of others. Give me sensitivity to their pain and rejoicing in their successes. Help me to treat others well.

Goodness

Make me good, Oh Lord. Give me the desire to do the things that I ought to do and avoid the things that I ought not to do.

Faithfulness

Grant me the belief and understanding that lets me stand in times of trouble—to hang tough and to know that You are God and I am not. And in the good times, Lord, help me not to forget You.

Gentleness

Give me compassion for others, the exact right touch for each situation, and a kind heart.

Self-Control

Provide in me the restraint that keeps all things in my life in harmony with You, Lord. Help me to walk straight, live with integrity, and keep up the good fight.

The Fruits of the Spirit are the ultimate in biblical sexiness. As you struggle to live them, you make yourself more appealing to your spouse, and you learn to live God's plan for your life. If you want to have fun with your clothes off, work on how you live with your clothes on.

We started with the Fruits of the Spirit. Now let's talk about some physical "good fruits."

Alcohol

Alcohol must be the most used aphrodisiac in the world. Why? Alcohol lowers inhibitions. Many people have sexual hang-ups. Drinking alcohol tends to relax people and put them more in the mood for a little rumpy-pumpy.

We can use alcohol to address a challenging Christian principle: What are we allowed to do?

Let me tell you a story. When I was in my late 20s, my co-worker, Jack, and I went to a bar together and got drunk. We laughed as we talked about our kids, our wives, and our work. We were good friends and brothers in the Lord. I remember barely being able to walk as we left the bar. A few days later, Jack called to tell me he was going into a 30-day alcohol rehabilitation program. As I prayed for him, I got a clear message (which I believe to be a directive from the Holy Spirit) that if Jack couldn't drink anymore, then neither could I. So I abstained from alcohol for over 25 years, and I never regretted the decision.

I didn't have a drinking problem like Jack did, but I did have a maturity problem. I needed time to grow into the man God wanted me to be. I'm still working on that. I knew, though, that God didn't want me drinking alcohol anymore. It was forbidden for me. But I recently felt a strong urging that I was too prideful about my abstinence—that an occasional drink would be right for me, even though I don't particularly enjoy drinking.

I like when Debby drinks, though, because her inhibitions go down. I don't really have any inhibitions. I'm thinking of asking for some for Christmas. Regardless of inhibitions, Debby and I both feel God gives us the grace to drink alcohol.

The Bible explains this principle of grace in different ways, but it's difficult for us to grasp. We tend to want simple rules. Grace tells us that everything is allowable, but the Holy Spirit will tell you what is permissible for you.[83] Jesus tells us not to judge others.[84] How could I possibly know what the Holy Spirit is telling you to do? Yet, we spend much of our

---

[83] I Corinthians 10:23-31 and I Corinthians 6:12
[84] Matthew 7:1-5

lives trying to manage the behavior of others. We all love bossing someone else around. It's easier to do that than to deal with our own issues.

Regarding alcohol, then, follow God's leading. But remember: alcohol may be poison for you, or it may be poison to your spouse; the struggle to abstain from alcohol may be so challenging for your spouse that your only reasonable response is to also abstain. The beautiful grace of Christianity lets you decide and live with the consequences.

Caution about alcohol-sex dependence: Be careful not to become dependent on alcohol for good sex. Remember that variety keeps sex fun for years. Don't get caught in the trap where good sex only occurs with alcohol onboard. If that tends to be the case in your marriage, figure out what the alcohol changes about you or your spouse's behavior and try to address it in another way.

For example, if your spouse tends to be tense and the alcohol acts as a relaxer, try a full body massage instead or watch a funny show that you both enjoy. Laughter works well as foreplay. On the other hand, perhaps your spouse feels on some deep level that sex is disgusting. Alcohol helps temporarily alleviate that feeling, but you don't want to always rely on alcohol for fun sex.

You may want to talk to a counselor or perhaps study a Song of Songs together. Perhaps study this book, *Great Sex, Christian Style,* together. I can't imagine being able to talk Debby into doing that, but it might work for you and your spouse. Remember, it can take considerable effort to understand the source of sexual hang-ups. And it takes even more effort to change them. You've got the time, though. Are you are willing to put in the effort?

Cannabis

Did I just lose half my readers with this subheading? If you're still here, let me help you "just say no" to fear thinking. Cannabis is legal in many states now and will likely soon be legal in many more. It is a life changing medicine for many folks.[85] For others, it simply provides a way to relax. As with any drug, though, it's bad medicine for some.

As the trend toward legalization continues, you may find that recreational cannabis spices up your love making. Our son, Lex Pelger, works as a drug writer

---

[85] Lex Pelger, "The War on Weed is a War on the Elderly," Ladybud, February 10, 2014, http://www.ladybud.com/2014/02/10/the-war-on-weed-is-a-war-on-the-elderly/.

and researcher. After conducting hundreds of interviews, he found a pattern of cannabis driving sexual desire…especially in women.

One woman in her 50s noted a downside of menopause being loss of libido. She couldn't get that "Off to the races" feeling anymore, but then she smoked a bit of hash for the first time in decades. She felt like she'd had a multi-orgasmic miracle. She says:

> When I smoke, the worries of the day and the plans for the next day vanish, which allows me to be truly present for having sex. It only takes two tokes; I don't need much. I try to do it at least once a week. For menopausal women, when you think you're done, it's a new lease on life.

Her 64-year-old husband added:

> When menopause came, our love life slowly faded. It was sad. We were loving, just not very sexual. Then she discovered the effects of cannabis and hash on her libido. To be able to pleasure my wife again, so ecstatically like before, meant the world to me. It makes growing older so much better.

Cannabis isn't just for us old-folks. Terence Mckenna, an advocate for the responsible use of naturally occurring psychedelic plants—called the Timothy Leary of the 1990s—spoke about the sexual stamina cannabis provides. As a young man, the thrill of sex was haunted for him by the fear of premature ejaculation. He said, "I discovered that smoking hashish gave me an incredible ability to control my ejaculation and also my sexual stamina...invaluable social skills."[86]

If you decide cannabis is something you want to try, the ingestion options have greatly improved from just rolling and smoking a joint. Edibles are simple, but can take up to two hours to kick in. That makes date night planning a bit more complicated. Also, the dosage of edibles is difficult to calibrate. You probably don't want to get uncomfortably stoned. If you use edibles, be cautious about dosage. You can always consume more but you can't un-consume.

Vape pens provide a great method to get high for sex. The vape pen warms the cannabis enough to release

---

[86] "Quotes from Terrence Mckenna," The Dope Smoker, April 25, 2011, http://www.dope-smoker.co.uk/quotes-from-terrance-mckenna/.

the psychoactive agents but not enough to burn. You inhale vapor but not smoke. Within a couple minutes of taking a puff, you will know exactly how high you are. You can also easily take another puff during the belly bumping.

The most challenging aspect of using cannabis as an aphrodisiac or as medicine is the dose variation. Start small and see how things feel.

On the other hand, time suspension seems the best benefit of cannabis during sex. The normal experience of time changes. Love making becomes a fascinating dance where pleasure and time roll together.

Chocolate

Let's look at something less controversial—something Debby and I both love: chocolate. I eat some wonderful dark chocolate every day to make myself happier and healthier. Drizzling dark chocolate on your spouse's naughty parts and licking it off is a fun way to use this aphrodisiac in your sex life. Maybe add a side of strawberries or blueberries. Have some healthy, messy fun with dark chocolate and fruit.

Or try a love making meal of chocolate fondue with fruits, breads, and cheeses:

- 3 oz chopped dark chocolate bar
- 1/2 cup natural cocoa powder
- 1/2 cup heavy cream
- 1 tablespoon sugar
- 1 tablespoon butter
- 1/2 teaspoon ground cinnamon

Mix and microwave for two minutes (or melt in a fondue pot). Then, find whatever you want to dip: strawberries, bananas, pretzels, pound cake, raspberries, pineapples, blueberries, angel food cake, etc. Consider sprinkling grated coconut on top (because everything is better with coconut). You could add some sliced almonds or anything else your crooked little heart desires.

Perhaps you want to have some hot cocoa to refresh you after one love making session to get you prepped for Round Two. Try this recipe for two servings:

- 1/3 cup natural cocoa powder
- 3 tablespoons of sugar
- Pinch salt

- 2 1/2 cups whole milk
- Whipped cream or marshmallows

Mix the dry ingredients and 1/4 cup of milk and whisk till smooth. Then add the rest of the milk and stir as you heat on the stove for a few minutes until hot (don't let it boil).

Adding a splash of vanilla will heighten the chocolate flavor, or add mint or cinnamon. Various types of liquor can also be added. You could even add a bit of butter browned to a pan...just don't do all these things at one time. Just like in sex, consider variety and timing.

I don't know if chocolate should really be considered an aphrodisiac or if it is just wonderful. I don't care. Chocolate makes life and sex better, so why not eat some?

Herbs and Supplements

When it comes to supplements, though, we probably need to be a bit more discerning than we are with our consumption of chocolate. There are dozens of herbs and supplements that have purported properties to aid in sex. None are proven. You may want to research some of these on your own and give one a try to see if it works for you.

The following supplements supposedly increase blood flow to the genital area, providing better erections for men and better orgasms for women. I've tried the first three and found them somewhat effective. Other folks have had the same experience. So much of sex is in your mind, though, so attaining scientific proof of the usefulness of an herbal aphrodisiac would be challenging.

1. **Ginseng root**: For centuries, people have written about the enhanced vitality, energy, and sex drive that comes from ingesting the ginseng root.
2. **L-Arginine**: This is thought to relax blood vessels and increase blood flow to the penis for better erections.
3. **Ginkgo Biloba**: This is a traditional Chinese medicine that is also thought to be able to relax blood vessels and increase blood flow to the penis for better erections.
4. **Yohimbe**: Extract from the bark of the African yohimbe tree, this traditional aphrodisiac may increase erections and libido.
5. **Pycnogenol**: This is extract from a French pine tree that seems to help produce nitric oxide, similar to L-arginine, yohimbe,

ginkgo, and ginseng. It is purported to be most effective when paired with L-arginine.

6. **Black Cohosh**: This seems to have estrogen-type properties and increases blood flow to the pelvis area, which means more lubrication—always a good thing. It is also marketed to help alleviate menopausal symptoms.

7. **Maca**: This is a Peruvian vegetable and traditional aphrodisiac.

8. **Zestra for Women**: This is a blend of oils and extracts that is applied directly on the clitoris.

9. **Vitamin E oil**: This can be applied to the vagina for increased lubrication.

The Arts and Senses

Does a certain kind of music put you or your spouse more in the mood? Pay attention to that. Try a Pandora station that comes up with similar songs automatically or make your own playlist. Be intentional about the music you play in the bedroom.

Or perhaps great art or sculptures get your motors running. I love Rodin's *The Kiss*. If you or your spouse are particularly invigorated by art, go on a date to a museum or watch a museum tour online.

Of course, visual stimulation doesn't need to be highbrow to be enjoyable. Debby and I enjoy simply paging through Vogue magazine and looking at the ads. Getting a look into the world of fashion can stimulate the senses for sex.

Smells are a powerful stimulator as well. Try burning incense or a scented candle or whatever seems good to you and your spouse. Think art, think senses, think beauty, and think fun.

Healthy Living

Another fantastic thing you can do for your sex life is eat healthy and live healthy. If your body is in good shape, your sex life has a better chance of being in good shape. Get adequate sleep, water, and exercise. Laugh often. If you feel invigorated often and live a life filled with joy, you'll be sexier.

There aren't any shortcuts for healthy living. You know what to do. If you don't do it, take a moment to think, "Why don't I do it"? Could better sex be a motivator for you to change some habits? It works for me.

Erection Pills

What about erectile dysfunction drugs such as Viagra, Cialis, or Levitra? I thought about trying them for book research, but the possible side effects—including headaches, heartburn, prolonged erections leading to penis damage and sudden onset hearing loss—deterred me.

However, if your sex life resembles something like, as my father would say, "Trying to stuff a marshmallow into a piggy bank," then you may want to see your doctor about erection pills. My advice, though? Don't use these drugs unless you *really* need them.

Great sex won't come from a pill. Mutual respect, love, silliness, spontaneity, intimate conversations, and a whole host of other activities and emotions lead to great sex. As Boston Globe columnist Ellen Goodman wrote, "I can't help wondering why we got a pill to help men with performance instead of communication." Like everything good in life, there really aren't any shortcuts to great sex.

Anti-Aphrodisiacs

To close this chapter, since we're discussing aphrodisiacs and performance enhancers, let's also consider what impedes good sex. Keeping with the overall theme of this chapter, I'll start with selfishness, laziness, and meanness. A surefire way to have a crappy sex life? Be a jerk.

Another anti-aphrodisiac is over-the-counter medications. Antihistamines, for example, may hinder a women's lubrication production. Other medications, antidepressants in particular, can lessen your desire for sex. Betty Dodson, author of the bestseller *Sex for One: The Joy of Self-Loving*, remained a sex writer and researcher into her 90s. She said, "Anti-depressants take away female orgasms. I'd be depressed too if no orgasms. You may want to try cannabis. It's the only aphrodisiac I recommend."[87]

Too much time spent on a bicycle seat can also cause some serious problems in your pants. If you are a fanatic cycler and things aren't working quite right below the belt, pay attention and talk to your doctor. I love to ride bike, but one of the reasons I do triathlons is the varied training, which keeps me from doing too much squishing of my schvontz in any one sport.

Many other physical and psychological issues cause sexual problems. Sorry, but those are above my pay

---

[87] Betty is quoted saying this in an interview with Lex Pelger. She also shared her advice on http://www.dodsonandross.com/ with the motto, "Better Orgasms. Better World."

grade. Talk to a doctor—or three—if you need that kind of help.

Chapter 6

I Just Want to be Biblical

I love the Bible. I've read through it many times. I make notes in the margins, ponder passages, and enjoy the truth as it wells up in me. Both my heart and my brain tell me the Bible is completely true. There's a big difference, though, between knowing the Bible to be true and assuming all that truth is clear to me.

In this chapter, we're going to consider various biblical texts and how the mainstream understanding of them has changed over time. When God gave me the idea to analyze what the Bible says about sex, he used many seemingly unrelated texts to guide me.

This Bible study may seem challenging, and it might appear to have nothing to do with sex, but be open to God showing you the threads that connect these passages—the threads I believe he showed me.

Hard to Understand Texts

When I read about the many times God commanded genocide, I struggle to reconcile how the God I know could do that.[88] When the Bible shows a clear support of slavery, I wonder on which side I would have been fighting in the American Civil War. I come across so many verses that make me wonder. For example:

> *If two men are fighting and the wife of one of them comes to rescue her husband from his assailant, and she reaches out and seizes him by his private parts, you shall cut off her hand. Show her no pity.*[89]

What conclusion am I supposed to draw from that passage? Don't mess with the package?

Many Bible verses baffle me. But that seems consistent with the world God created. After all, he made 350,000 species of beetles, which is more than all the plant and mammal species combined. Why did God go wild on beetle creation? We won't find an answer in the Bible, and I'm fine with that…in fact I like it. I'd hate to live in a world that someone as silly as me could understand.

I know I don't want God asking me the questions he mockingly asked Job.

---

[88] Joshua 6:20-21, Deuteronomy 2:32-35, Numbers 31:7-18
[89] Deuteronomy 25:11-12

Where were you when I laid the earth's foundation? Tell me, if you understand. Who marked off its dimensions? Surely you know! Who stretched a measuring line across it? On what were its footings set, or who laid its cornerstone—while the morning stars sang together and all the angels shouted for joy?[90]

To understand the Bible's message about sex, let's study a seemingly unrelated topic: slavery. Please hang with me as we delve into slavery to glean the parallels to sex.

Slavery

The Bible applies perfectly to all its readers in ancient times, in modern times, and all times in between. In order for that to be true, though, some passages need to be read within their unique cultural context. For example, Paul writes:

Slaves, obey your earthly masters with respect and fear, and with sincerity of heart, just as you would obey Christ.
Obey them not only to win their favor when their eye is on you, but as slaves of Christ, doing the will of God from your heart.
Serve wholeheartedly, as if you were serving the Lord, not people.[91]

---

[90] Job 38:4-7
[91] I Pet 2:17-20 (NIV 2011)

In this passage, he references the current laws and standards. Slavery wasn't a controversial issue of social justice in ancient times. It was the normal way of life. If you weren't a slave, you were probably part of a household that owned slaves. A slave wasn't just property; wives and children were also property. A slave was a slave for life, alienated, treated with violence, and generally dishonored.[92]

In this culture where slavery was normal, Paul instructs slaves how to act. Few of us believe Paul was writing a rule for all future cultures. That distinction will be important later as we analyze biblical texts on sex.

Jesus also makes reference to servants (i.e., slaves) in his parables. Neither Jesus, nor Paul, nor any Biblical writer ever mentions opposition to the institution of slavery.[93] As we saw in the above, New Testament writers told slaves how to be better slaves, not how to escape or change the slavery system.

---

[92] Orlando Patterson, *Slavery and Social Death* (Cambridge MA: Harvard College, 1982), 13.

[93] You could argue that Paul told the owner of Onesimus to give him his freedom to help Paul, but that wasn't an argument against the institution of slavery itself.

The Old Testament supports slavery even more. Moses, the lawgiver, describes how slaves can be purchased and handed down as property.[94]

> *Your male and female slaves are to come from the nations around you; from them you may buy slaves.*
>
> *You may also buy some of the temporary residents living among you and members of their clans born in your country, and they will become your property.*
>
> *You can bequeath them to your children as inherited property and can make them slaves for life, but you must not rule over your fellow Israelites ruthlessly.[95]*

Most folks today who read the hundreds of pro-slavery verses in the Bible conclude that these writings were meant to be taken in cultural context.[96] Certainly God does not command slavery or even endorse it. He allowed comments to be made about a current practice.

But, if you lived in the American South in the mid-1800s, owned slaves, and loved Jesus, you likely

---

[94] Abraham, the great man of faith in the Bible, was also a slave owner (Gen 12:5). Solomon writes that slaves will need to be beaten for correction (Prov 29:19).

[95] Leviticus 25:44-46

[96] Supposedly 326 pro-slavery Bible verses, though I haven't counted.

would have interpreted these Bible verses differently. How could these Northern agitators—the so-called abolitionists—conclude that God was on their side?

In fact, even Christian slaves struggled with how to interpret biblical teachings on slavery. Frederick Douglass, who was born a slave and escaped north in his mid-20s, wrote, "I had at times asked myself the question, 'May not my condition after all be God's work, ordered for a wise purpose, and if so, is not submission my duty?'" [97]

Douglass struggled with the concept of being a "slave for life." In his younger years, he accepted the brutality he encountered, but the thought that he would never be anything but someone else's property—never have a permanent wife, never be certain when his children would be sold away from him—made that life unbearable.

Douglass decided to escape. He expected to be tortured and to die. He consciously chose death over a continued life of slavery. He knew slavery was a great evil, both to the slaves and to the slave holders, but he'd heard the pro-slave verses preached as truth his entire life.

---

[97] Douglass, Frederick, *The Life and Times of Frederick Douglass*, (Mineola, NY: Dover Publications, Inc, 2003), 141.

Now let's try to imagine what our life might be like in America in the 1850s as a slave. The master could rape you (though it's not rape because you're his property). The master could make you work anywhere and take all your wages. The master could sell your children. The master was not allowed by law to teach you to read. The master could kill you.

On the other hand, say you lived in the North. You probably didn't think about slavery often. It was an issue far away that affected other people. You're busy enough with your own life and don't need to solve other people's problems. No one made you the General Manager of the Universe.

But if you lived in the South and weren't a slave, you grew up with slavery being a normal part of the culture. Your minister preached regularly on pro-slavery verses. You believed the kindest thing you could do for the colored folks was to keep them in slavery since they weren't capable of taking care of themselves.

How would you have interpreted the Bible if you were in one of these situations above in the 1850s? How would you have lived? Would you have said about slavery, "The Bible says it, I believe it and that settles it"? Or would you have been an abolitionist?

Most abolitionists were ardent Christians who felt the Holy Spirit leading them to declare slavery evil and fight against it. Douglass writes about the Quakers who helped him gain freedom at great risk to themselves.[98] He marvels at those who "took me in when I was a stranger" and "fed me when I was hungry." Douglass (and all slaves eventually) felt the love of Jesus through those works.

Jesus gave us a simple test. Every good tree bears good fruit, but a bad tree bears bad fruit.[99] William Wilberforce showed the bad fruits of slavery to the British Empire in the early 1800s. The American Abolitionists highlighted those bad fruits in the mid-1800s, culminating in the Civil War. As the laws changed, churches evaluated the scriptural teaching vs the bad fruits concept.

Slavery was a case in which biblical interpretation and church doctrine changed dramatically. What are some others?

Church Changes Over Time

Here are a few examples in which the Church argued, fought, and changed:

1. **All believers must be circumcised and follow the dietary laws**.[100] Paul, Peter, and James pushed to eliminate the requirement for new male believers to be circumcised and

---

[98] Ibid. 143-4.
[99] Matthew 7:15-20
[100] Acts 15:1-29

eat Kosher. No one debates this in Christianity today.

2. **The sun and stars revolve around the Earth.** [101] Galileo paid the price for this change by spending his life following his 1633 conviction for heresy under house arrest. No non-nitwits dispute the scientific proof against this one.

3. **The Earth is about 6,000 years old.** Since the early Church, religious scholars counted the years in the genealogies and stipulated a year of creation and of Christ's second coming. Even Isaac Newton, in the early 1700s, worked on an Earth chronology with the 6,000-year assumption. Then James Hutton, the father of modern geology, realized the Earth is much older. [102] Most scientists today agree the Earth is about 4.6 billion years old, though some Christians still hold to the 6,000-year age.

4. **Everything has been the subject of debate.** Musical instruments, types of music, styles of dress, Sunday School, alcohol, tobacco and many other things have been debated in the Church over the years since Christ's resurrection.

---

[101] Psalms 93:1, Psalms 96:10, Psalms 104:5, I Chronicles 16:30, Joshua 10:13, and Ecclesiastes 1:5

[102] Jack Repcheck, *The Man Who Found Time*, (New York, NY: Basic Books of Perseus Books Group, 2009), 152. Jack is my grandson's other grandfather.

What are we fighting about now? Acceptance of homosexuality is a big one. When people are asked about their impressions of Christians, they generally don't talk about our amazing charity. They see us as judgmental, hypocritical, anti-homosexual, and boring.[103] Much of that sentiment comes back to homosexuality.

Most Christians believe the Bible states clearly that homosexuality is a sin. That's what I thought. Then a friend asked me if I remembered the first time I saw a Playboy magazine. I did. I remembered that strong attraction and something funny going on in my pants. I was like, "Stand back, I don't know how big this thing is gonna get." Turns out I had nothing to worry about.

But then my friend asked me to consider if I would have had that sexual attraction when I saw men in a magazine. I realized I didn't make a choice to be attracted to women, I just was. I started to feel empathy for the folks who felt same sex attraction and were told it's a sin. I decided to read the entire Bible, paying close attention to sex and marriage.

---

[103] David Kinnaman and Gabe Lyons, "unChristian: What a New Generation Really Thinks About Christianity... And Why It Matters," www1.cbn.com/books/what-non-christians-really-think-of-us.

Clobber Verses

I took two years to carefully read through the Bible and take prodigious notes. Let's have a look at what I found. We'll start with a cheery topic: sodomy.

Ask most Christians about Sodom and Gomorrah and you'll hear that God destroyed the city because the people were engaging in homosexual behavior. Read the story in Genesis 19, though, and you'll see it is a commentary on mob mentality and rape. Lot offered his virgin daughters to the mob to be raped in order to spare his guests.

To our modern minds, Lot's offer appalls us, but we learned in chapter 2 about the Greco-Roman world's emphasis on community honor and shame. For Lot to have allowed his guests to be raped would have brought great shame on his household and community. The low value of women in the patriarchal society was also a factor.

The sin of the mob (and of Sodom and Gomorrah) was meanness—a lack of compassion, kindness, and empathy for others. The eight times the New Testament references "Sodom" lack any mention of homosexual behavior. The biblical story of Sodom simply isn't about homosexuality.

On the other hand, the Old Testament law commands men who engage in same sex relations be put to death.[104] We've all heard homosexuality called an "abomination."[105] But what else does the Bible call an "abomination"?

1. Eating ham, bacon, sausage, lobster, clams, shrimp, etc.[106]
2. Charging interest on a loan.[107]
3. Burning incense.[108]

The list of prohibitions is even wilder, including combinations of clothing, planting different plants next to one another, and engaging in sex during menstruation.

Matthew Vines in *God and the Gay Christian* goes beyond the simple debate of whether to ignore Old Testament laws and masterfully covers the complex issue of what modern Christians can learn from Old Testament law.[109] If you want to go deeper into this topic, read his book. In this book, however, I'm content to know I'm not bound by all those Old Testament laws. And that's good, because I really love bacon.

---

[104] Leviticus 18:22 and Leviticus 20:13

[105] The "abomination" language is found in the King James Version in Leviticus 20:13.

[106] Leviticus 11:9-12

[107] Ezekiel 18:13

[108] Isaiah 1:13

[109] Matthew Vines, *God and the Gay Christian: The Biblical Case in Support of Same-Sex Relationships* (New York, NY, Convergent Books, 2014), 77.

Now let's evaluate the most challenging of the clobber verses from Romans 1:

> *Because of this, God gave them over to shameful lusts. Even their women exchanged natural relations for unnatural ones. In the same way the men also abandoned natural relations with women and were inflamed with lust for one another. Men committed indecent acts with other men, and received in themselves the due penalty for their perversion.*[110]

When you read that, you likely conclude that Paul makes it clear that Homosexuality is sinful. But take the time to read the rest of that section of Romans: 1:18-32.

In the rest of the chapter, Paul makes the key point that people tend to not put God first. They tend to worship idols—anything that one loves more than God. Then Paul gives the example—not a command—about sex becoming an idol.

The true sexual sin of the times was excess—failing to have the moderation that was required of an elite man. Excess passion was considered weak and womanly. Here's a first century quote from Dio Chrysostom that provides cultural context:

---

[110] Rom 1:26-27

The man whose appetite is insatiate in such things (referring to sex with women), when he finds there is no scarcity, no resistance, in this field, will have contempt for the easy conquest and scorn for a woman's love, as a thing too readily given—in fact, too utterly feminine—and will turn his assault against the male quarters, eager to befoul the youth who will very soon be magistrates and judges and generals, believing that in them he will find a kind of pleasure difficult and hard to procure.[111]

Dio then describes wine drinkers who become addicted and go to extremes. For both sex and alcohol, moderate use was appropriate and extreme use a problem.

Paul writes from this same cultural context. He uses homo-erotic sex as an example of failing to be satisfied with moderation and making sex an idol above God. In Paul's patriarchal culture, homosexuality as we recognize it today didn't exist.[112] While plenty of homo-erotic activity went on, we don't find any record of the kind of committed, same-sex relationships we see today. Paul wasn't making a law against something that didn't exist.

---

[111] Dio Chrysostom, "The seventh or Euboean Discourse," last page.

[112] Joseph A. Marchal, "Homosexual/Queer," in *The Oxford Encyclopedia of the Bible and Gender Studies,* ed. Julia M. O'Brien (New York: Oxford University Press, 2014), Volume 1, p. 340.

As you read Romans 1:26, perhaps the word "unnatural" is what bothers you most. You probably visualize how a penis fits into a vagina and think that's natural, so anything else must be unnatural. But when you consider the amazing complexity of God's creation, do you really want to base this important decision about what is right or wrong concerning sexuality on your need to keep things simple? Think about it: Paul wrote that homo-erotic sex was unnatural, but he wrote the same thing about men having long hair. Sorry, hipsters.

The most compelling reason for me to reject the idea that Romans 1 is a clear biblical rule against homosexuality comes in the verses that follow it.

> *They have become filled with every kind of wickedness, evil, greed and depravity. They are full of envy, murder, strife, deceit and malice. They are gossips, slanderers, God-haters, insolent, arrogant and boastful; they invent ways of doing evil; they disobey their parents; they are senseless, faithless, heartless, ruthless.*[113]

I commit many of those sins. I am occasionally wicked and often greedy. I gossip and have been known to disobey my parents. Sometimes I realize I've been heartless and ruthless. The amazing grace

---

[113] Rom 1:29-31

of God gives me hope that I am loved even in my sinful existence.

Paul isn't trying to make us hate homosexuals in Romans 1; he wants us to recognize the kinds of behavior that lead us away from God. He wants us to put God first in our lives. Any of the sins of excess and idolatry make it difficult for us to put God first. That is Paul's point.

Let's move now to the last clobber verse: the catalog of sins. Since the translation matters so much, we'll start with the King James Version, the earliest of the modern translations:

> *Know ye not that the unrighteous shall not inherit the kingdom of God? Be not deceived: neither fornicators, nor idolaters, nor adulterers, nor effeminate, nor abusers of themselves with mankind, Nor thieves, nor covetous, nor drunkards, nor revilers, nor extortioners, shall inherit the kingdom of God.[114]*

Paul wrote this letter to help the young, struggling church in Corinth develop holiness—to live moral and God-focused lives. Immediately prior to the verses shown above, Paul tells the church that the fact that they are suing each other means they are already defeated. He challenges them to submit to the

---

[114] I Cor 6:9-10 KJV

injustice—even to allow themselves to be cheated—rather than sue. Then Paul describes ten types of wicked people and concludes that their conduct will keep them from inheriting God's kingdom. Let's go through that list and see how we fair:

1. **Fornicators**: This is the Greek word *Pornea*, explained previously, which is a non-specific word for sexual sins. Jesus stipulated that looking with lust at another woman is a sexual sin...I'm already in trouble.

2. **Idolaters**: The best definition for this seems to be putting anything in our lives ahead of God—yet another test most of us fail.

3. **Adulterers**: This is the Greek word *Moichos*, which means sex outside marriage for a woman or a man having sex with a married woman who is not his wife. Hopefully few of us fail this one.

4. **Effeminate**: This is the Greek word *Malokoi*, which seems to mean "softness." It was used to describe "men who acted effeminately" against the patriarchal culture that required strong and self-controlled men.[115] One commentator described the term as an ancient equivalent of telling a boy he "throws like a

---

[115] Lynn R. Huber, "Same-Sex Relations: New Testament," in *The Oxford Encyclopedia of the Bible and Gender Studies,* ed. Julia M. O'Brien (New York: Oxford University Press, 2014), Volume 2, p. 277.

girl."[116] If you're less than a manly man, you may fail this one…I don't.

5. **Abusers of themselves with mankind**: The Greek word for this, *Arsenokoites*, is not used anywhere else in the Bible and almost nowhere else in ancient literature. It seems Paul combined two words to create *Arsenokoites*: *Arseno* means male; *Koites* means bed. No one can definitively say what the word means, but the NIV translates it as "homosexual offenders." "Male prostitute" may be a better translation, though, since the few times it's used elsewhere it seems to be grouped with economic sins.[117] It couldn't have meant "homosexuals" since that concept wasn't developed until the late 1800s.

6. **Thieves**: A thief is someone who steals. This is another category in which we all miss the mark.

7. **Covetous**: It is defined as wanting what others have or being greedy. Every person I've ever met has been covetous.

---

[116] Eric Thurman, "Gender Transgression: Roman World," in *The Oxford Encyclopedia of the Bible and Gender Studies,* ed. Julia M. O'Brien (New York: Oxford University Press, 2014), Volume 1, p. 298.

[117] Lynn R. Huber, "Same-Sex Relations: New Testament," in *The Oxford Encyclopedia of the Bible and Gender Studies,* ed. Julia M. O'Brien (New York: Oxford University Press, 2014), Volume 2, p. 276.

8. **Drunkards**: A few teetotalers can say they never fall into this category, but most folks fail here on occasion.
9. **Revilers**: The NIV translates this as "slanderers," so if we sometimes say things we wish we hadn't, we probably fail in this category.
10. **Extortioners**: The NIV translates this as "swindlers," which seems to involve the use of one's own power to take advantage of others. You probably only fail on this one if you have any power.

Read through that list again. Is it as clear to you as it is to me that no one deserves to inherit the kingdom of Heaven? Any thoughtful Christian already knows this. We live with our sinful nature every day. We treasure grace because it allows us to transcend who we are and become who we are capable of being.

I'm amazed that these verses are still used to keep people who identify as LGBTQ out of the church. The idea that two members of the same sex could be in a committed relationship only became known as a part of culture in the late 1800s. In G-R times, same sex behavior was just another way for an elite man to have his sexual needs met. The Bible, read in cultural context, couldn't have been prohibiting something that wasn't known to the culture itself. So, looking at those clobber verses, how might we respond to people who attempt to use them to exclude LGBTQ people? Here's a cheat sheet:

CLOBBER	RESPONSE
1. Sodom was destroyed for its homosexual behavior. (Genesis 19)	The story of Sodom and Gomorrah is about rape and a lack of compassion, kindness, and empathy. Sodom is not about homosexuality.
2. Homosexuality is an abomination to God. (Leviticus 20)	So is ham, bacon, and lobster...so is charging interest on a loan and burning incense. There are far more OT prohibitions that simply don't apply to Christians, and homosexuality is one of them.
3. Homosexual behavior is shameful and unnatural. (Romans 1)	This is an example Paul is using to discourage idolatry. It is not a command or a new law. This caution against idolatry (putting anything else above God) also applies to greed, gossip, and a whole host of other things we all do on a regular basis.
4. Homosexuality is a sin. (1 Corinthians 6 or Ephesians 5)	The words used in these verses couldn't have been referring to homosexuality as that concept only developed in the late 1800s. The purpose of this list is to show us all that as sinners, we cannot inherit God's Kingdom apart from the grace of Christ.

How Jesus Changed Marriage

Prior to Jesus, the main purpose of marriage was to produce legitimate, male heirs.[118] The male head of the household wanted to be able to pass his assets down to his own children. Marriages were contracts between families. The government was not involved in marriage in any way. Marriage was not an "institution." Marriages tended to be utilitarian and many ended in death or divorce.[119]

Divorce was simply the nullification of a contract. It was common and simple. If the wife brought a dowry (her inheritance from her father given to her husband at marriage) into the marriage, she was generally allowed to take it with her when she left. Though if the males in the family agreed on her infidelity, she would forfeit her dowry.[120]

Jesus preached a less utilitarian and more spiritual view of marriage. He made it the "ideal" for a couple to stay married for life. He said several times that a man who divorces his wife and marries another

---

[118] B. Diane Lipsett, "Marriage and Divorce: Early Church," in *The Oxford Encyclopedia of the Bible and Gender Studies* ed. Julia M. O'Brien (New York: Oxford University Press, 2014), Volume 1, p. 506.

[119] Julie Langford, "Marriage and Divorce: Roman World," in *The Oxford Encyclopedia of the Bible and Gender Studies* ed. Julia M. O'Brien (New York: Oxford University Press, 2014), Volume 1, p. 495.

[120] Ibid. 496.

commits adultery.[121] While some believers take this to be a rule against remarriage, those same believers likely do not require adherence to Jesus' command to the rich young man to sell everything and give it to the poor.[122]

Jesus changed marriage, and the world, not by making rules but by teaching us a new way to live. Rather than keeping divorce easy and common, Jesus encouraged his followers to hang in and work through the problems that come up in marriage. Jesus showed us how to love others in a sacrificial way, rather than sticking to the idea that marriage was for the sole purpose of producing heirs. Jesus' teachings made marriages last longer and stay stronger.

Some of his early followers in the first few hundred years of church history made other marriage rules:

1. Sex is only for procreation.
2. Even procreation sex shouldn't be enjoyed, only tolerated.
3. All must remain celibate.
4. Masturbation is forbidden.
5. Homo-erotic sex is forbidden.

Most of these rules have been deemed wrong over time. Some early Christian writers, though, seemed to understand Jesus' true intention. Tertullian wrote

---

[121] Mark 10:2-12, Matthew 19:1-9, I Corinthians 7
[122] Mark 10:17-21

this lovely passage outlining a new view of marriage in "To His Wife":

> Side by side in the Church of God and at the banquet of God, side by side in difficulties, in times of persecution and in times of consolation. Neither hides anything from the other, neither shuns the other, neither is a burden to the other. They freely visit the sick and sustain the needy. They give alms without anxiety, attend the sacrifice without scruple, perform their daily duties unobstructed. [123]

That shared, holy purpose and friendship between spouses came out of Jesus' teachings about marriage. The Romans moved things in that direction, making marital monogamy the law, but the Christian *agape* love changed marriage and changed the world.

Unfortunately, many Christians in the early church, and up to present day, continued to hold on to patriarchy and legalism, despite Jesus spending so much time speaking against legalism and hypocrisy. I think Jesus grieves when his followers make rules for others instead of showing agape love. Let's look at another act most of us were taught was un-Christian.

---

[123] Tertullian, "To His Wife," in *Miscellanies 2.23.*

Masturbation

Many Christians judge masturbation to be sinful, yet no biblical prohibition exists. In fact, The Bible hardly mentions masturbation at all.

In Genesis 38:8-10, Onan has sex with his dead brother's wife (per custom) but pulls out and spills his "seed" on the ground so Tamar won't get pregnant. He doesn't want to share his inheritance with the child that would result from the union. He didn't masturbate, but it was coitus interruptus. He was punished because he was selfish.

There are also stories about God's bride, Jerusalem, melting down gold, silver, and jewels to make male idols with which to act promiscuously.[124] The fact that Ezekiel wrote this presumably means that his readers were familiar with the concept of a dildo. Remember, in these times, women were thought unable to control their passions.

The OT Law mentions wet dreams as making one unclean till evening.[125] This again seems to be treated as a normal occurrence. No Biblical ban on masturbation exists. But the lack of a ban doesn't necessarily make it good either. Just recognize here that any teaching that masturbation is "sinful according to the Bible" is not accurate.

---

[124] Ezekiel 16:17 and 23:7
[125] Leviticus 15:16-17

We've talked about the difficult to understand texts of the Bible in their cultural contexts. We've explored the ways in which ideas about slavery, homosexuality, patriarchy, and masturbation have changed, failed to change over time, or never really existed with any concrete evidence. Now let's look at one concept that has remained consistent since Christ, Paul, and countless other biblical and non-canonical writers taught about it: lust. If you want to be biblical in your sex life, you can't avoid discussing lust.

The Sin of Lust

While Jesus gave us a new view of marriage, he also clearly named lust a sexual sin. What did he mean by the sin of lust? When I look obsessively at a woman, seeing her as a tasty little morsel and not as a sacred human being, I commit the sin of lust, and it cheapens the amazing life God has given me.

The females being objectified know that I am a creep; they can feel it. It reminds me of the way the Devil looked at victims in *The Screwtape Letters* by C.S. Lewis: as treats to feed one's depravity. If you haven't read *The Screwtape Letters*, put this book down and go read it. Here's a quote from the senior Demon, Screwtape, to his nephew, Wormwood, a Junior Tempter:

> It does not matter how small the sins are, provided that their cumulative effect is to edge the man away from the Light and out into the Nothing. Murder is no better than cards if cards can do the trick. Indeed the safest road to Hell is the gradual one—the gentle slope, soft underfoot, without sudden turnings, without milestones, without signposts.[126]

Don't pretend the sin of lust isn't a big deal. Just like greed and envy, the gentle slope of sin can create a great gulf between you and God. Try to be like Job. He made a covenant with his eyes to not look lustfully at a young woman.[127] Job pleased God by striving to avoid lust. I want to be like Job...except for all that struggling and pain stuff.

Read in context, the Bible has a lot to teach about sex and culture. But remember: Jesus taught us to love God and love one another above all other commands. When you're striving to remain biblical in your sex life, remember to read the verses we discussed in their cultural context. Cascade other people with love...don't clobber them with judgement.

---

[126] C. S. Lewis, *The Screwtape Letters* (Middlesex, England: The Penguin Group, 1988), 65.
[127] Job 31:1-4

Chapter 7

Getting Handy: Fingers as Sex Toys

Do you remember when you first put your hands on someone else's genitals? How did you feel? Excited, guilty, intrigued, or clumsy? I was mostly clumsy, like the little Dutch boy trying to plug a hole in the dyke.

I'm sure it was uncomfortable for my partner. Of course, I was too embarrassed to ask. Given the amazing complexity of our hands, it's a shame we don't tend to know how to best utilize them. This chapter will teach you to turn your paws into pleasure tools...or at least you'll learn how others do it.

Female Stimulation

Let's start with female stimulation and quotes from *The Guide to Getting it On*:

> Men make a big mistake when they forget to give their fingers a sense of humor. Fingertips that tease and dance will find an especially warm welcome between a woman's legs...It's not a dish

of salted peanuts down there, don't just grab and hope for the best.[128]

Let's begin by reviewing what we learned about the vulva in chapters 1 and 3. Can you draw the picture?

1. **Vagina opening** is at the center of the clock
2. **Mons Pubis** at 12:00
3. **Perineum** (located between vagina and anus) at 6:00
4. **Outer lips and inner lips** on either side
5. **Clitoral hood** located at the top of the inner lips
6. **Clitoris** under the hood

Seriously, can you draw this picture? Grab a pen and blank paper and let's play a little game of erotic Pictionary. If you want to see my sketch, go to GreatSexChristianStyle.com and have a gander.

So, we know the terrain; let's discuss objectives. Best to start with what your objectives aren't. You *aren't* on an orgasm race. Don't go right to the clitoris and start rubbing. You will be tempted to do that, because that's how most men masturbate: grab it hard and whack it good. Not to put too fine a point on this, but DON'T DO THIS TO A WOMAN.

---

[128] Paul Joannides, *Guide to Getting It On: A Book About the Wonders of Sex* (Oregon: Goofy Foot Press, 2014), 206.

Great sex will be spontaneous and creative. It will be different every time. But the basics remain the basics. When approaching hand play in the vulva area, the clitoris should be one of the last things you touch. In fact, don't even start in the vulva area. How about I give you a play-by-play of just one way to get there?

Start by offering to give her a massage. A massage is rarely turned down, even if the offer is clearly and wildly self-serving. Rub her back gently over her shirt, then begin kneading the muscles a bit harder. Ask what feels good and what hurts. After massaging longer than you want to, ask if you can take off her blouse and bra and start your skin on skin massage. Baby powder or massage oil work well here, but neither is required.

Make sure to work the shoulder and neck muscles. Rub down her arms and massage each hand and finger. Take your time; enjoy making her feel good.

Then start massaging her scalp. This is one of the keys to a great sensual massage: work through her hair rubbing her temples, the back, top, and front of her head, and down the neck.

Now massage down her back a bit and remove her pants and panties. Rub her butt and down each leg. Rub her feet, taking as much time with her feet as you did with her scalp.

When you complete each foot, go over her entire backside from scalp to back. Lightly and playfully touch and rub all the way up and down her naked back.

Then, help her turn over to lay on her back. Resist the temptation to dive right into your favorite part. Instead, start to massage her scalp again, which will feel different from this position. Gently rub her forehead, temples, cheeks, lips, chin, etc. This face massage should be relaxing and loving.

Tell her how beautiful she is and how lucky you feel to be with her. Then kiss her. Kiss her like you would if you were still in high school. Have fun making out for a while, then get back to massage.

Rub her shoulders, her arms, her hands, her chest, and her breasts. Gently rub her nipples and...wait a second, take a deep breath and calm down.

Move away from her breasts. Massage your way down her belly, understanding that many people tend to be embarrassed by their stomachs. Don't go to the vulva yet. Work your way down each leg. Again, provide a good quad, knee, calf, and foot massage. Then tickle, touch, tease, and massage your way back up to the vulva.

Even now, don't go right to the clitoris. Kneeling between her legs, start with a genital massage. Gently knead and rub around the clock face. Massage the mons pubis, thigh/outer lips, perineum, thigh/outer lips and back to the Mons pubis. Maybe make a few passes around there, slowly working your way toward the center.

Hopefully this sensual massage has her aroused. You may find plenty of natural lubrication down there or you may need to add some lube. Make sure not to touch the clitoris without plenty of "slipperiness."

Considering the need for lubrication on the clitoris: think about going down a waterslide that isn't wet…unpleasant, right? Don't stroke a dry clitoris.

The actual clitoral stimulation that feels best for your partner will vary. Try a light circular motion or an up stroke and a down stroke or a few fingers gently brushing upwards along the entire vulva. Try gently squeezing, rolling, or tapping. Again, take your time. Have fun. Try to determine if she's having fun.

One way to assess her arousal is to check for lubrication. Female lubrication varies. It varies a lot. Some women will produce a geyser of lubrication when they are aroused and others will remain dry. That varies further with the timing of the menstrual cycle and in menopause. As always, remember the importance of good lubrication, whether naturally produced or Passion Lube, saliva, KY Jelly, etc.

Ask her to tell you what feels good, but don't be surprised if she won't. Many women struggle to put their sexual feelings into words—probably from generations of inherited ideas that women should only act as sperm receptacles.

So here's an opportunity to not be a jerk. Your first assumption may be that she knows exactly what she wants or likes and won't tell you out of some spite. While that may happen sometimes, the more likely truth is that what she's feeling is so complex, she doesn't have easy answers to your questions.

Without being too sexist, it's fair to acknowledge that the female body and brain are more complex than the male. The plumbing necessary to have children (and the circuitry to nurture the little beggars as they scream late at night) makes for more complexity. Try to remember during sex, and in all your other interactions, that the female is in many ways fundamentally different from the male. Hopefully you're appreciating some of them during sex.

Ok, jumping off my pulpit and back to the hand work illustration. The instructions above give you some ideas to try, but the joy of great sex comes from variation. You're not opening a safe here; you're trying to love and connect with a God-created woman. Have fun with the options and possibilities. Here are a few other things to consider in the play:

Ask her to show you how she masturbates. Rest your hand above hers to gain a tactile understanding. You may want to try this while lying beside her so your hand works the same way hers does in that position.

Now let's consider vaginal penetration. Think of the vagina as a 4" long tube, like a cardboard toilet paper roll. Don't just go jamming your fingers in there like a piston. Again, try to be subtle. Go in one finger joint deep and gently touch at the 12:00 position, then work around the clock face.

Remember the vagina has pleasure receptors that are pressure-sensitive, so try varying pressures and motions to see what feels good to her. Keep in mind that the first third of the vagina tends to be most sensitive (great news for small penised men everywhere). You may then want to try going two finger joints deep. Remember to be playful. See what works. Have fun.

While you're in there, you're going to want to see if massaging her G spot causes pleasure or discomfort. It varies widely between women, so discard your preconceived notion and discover her truth.

To find the G spot area, massage the top of the vaginal wall with a "Come here" motion. Using one or two fingers in the vagina, making gentle upward circles, will locate that somewhat rough patch called the G spot. Another way to find the G spot is to put your thumb on her clitoris, insert your index finger and rub the rough spot on the upper vaginal wall.

For me, though, it seems a bit like trying reach up through the front grill of a car to open the hood latch. I'm in there feeling around but never seem to get the hood open. Don't fixate on the G Spot unless it works for her.

Back to the general topic of female stimulation. I've emphasized gentle touching and restrained hand play. You may find, though, that your partner likes two or three fingers in there (or even a fist) and some intense jamming. There are no rules for hand play, though you should go for subtlety until you learn otherwise.

If the info above is Female Stimulation 101 and you want to try a higher level course, check out a website completely dedicated to research and instruction for female orgasms: OMGYes.com.[129] They have videos and detailed instructions for the following strategies:

1. **Edging**: bringing about a bigger orgasm by approaching & denying
2. **Hinting**: passing by and only occasionally indulging

---

[129] https://www.omgyes.com/. I signed up by paying a one-time fee of $29.99 and had immediate access to all the videos and instructions on the 12 techniques. Everything on the website was impressive.

3. **Consistency**: keeping everything exactly the same
4. **Surprise**: defying expectation to enhance pleasure
5. **Rhythm**: a well-timed, almost musical, loop of motion
6. **Multiples**: overcoming sensitivity to build multiple orgasms
7. **Accenting**: paying extra attention to part of a motion
8. **Framing**: how pleasure is mostly between the ears
9. **Layering**: indirect pleasure through surrounding skin
10. **Staging**: ways sensitivity changes over time
11. **Orbiting**: the million ways of circling the clit
12. **Signaling**: styles of giving and receiving feedback

For a reasonable fee, you can get detailed instructions and listen to testimonials from women about each of these methods. Whether you're pre-orgasmic or just want more and better orgasms, I recommend you and your spouse give this a try.

Male Stimulation

Now let's transition to hand play on men. I've mentioned several times in previous chapters that male masturbation tends toward "Grab it hard and whack it good." So is that the best approach for a woman to take to satisfy her lover? Not necessarily.

Try for a higher standard. Think how much he'd appreciate some amazing hand job techniques. Think about the possibility of providing manual pleasure beyond his own masturbation methods...beyond "if you use your left hand, it feels like someone else is doing it."

I've borrowed heavily from the *Pleasure Mechanics* for this section.[130] Their video titled "Male Arousal Part 1: Handjobs" provides a visual instruction guide for pleasuring a man.[131] Here's a taste of their instructions for how to touch and stimulate a penis. I put this in list format and included many of my own ideas as well.

Warming up the penis: Get blood flowing for maximum sensitivity and firmest erections.

1. **Position**: Start by sitting between his legs, facing him. You may want to sit on a stool or chair and have him sit on the edge of the bed or sofa.
2. **Preparation**: Have a lubricant ready (silicon based Passion Lube, KY Jelly, or even coconut oil work well) and a cloth under him or sheets that you don't mind getting lubey.
3. **Finger and Thumb Massage**: Start at the penis base and knead with finger and thumb on either side of the penis. Work up slowly and come to just below the head before

---

[130] http://www.pleasuremechanics.com/.

[131] http://www.pleasuremechanics.com/foreplay-mastery/.

working back down. Continue this on other sides of the penis—up, then down. This isn't a particularly erotic feeling, but it massages penis tissue and gets blood flowing into it.

4. **Penis Stretches**: Gently pull the penis up to the belly, stretching the connecting tissue. This is the noon position; pull the penis over to 3:00, 6:00, 9:00 and back to noon. If you know how to drive a manual transmission, try shifting up and down the gears. Again, don't take too long with this, as it isn't overly erotic, but get the blood flowing. This might be a chance to laugh together at some silly fun.

5. **Thumb Circles**: Start at the base of the penis with both thumbs on his shaft. Rotate your right thumb clockwise and your left thumb counterclockwise. Think *Karate Kid*: wax on, whacks off. Slowly move up the penis shaft, continuing the thumb circles, and massage the penis tissue deeply. Stop just below the head. Remember, we are still in the warm up stage. When you get to the head, gently trail a finger down either side of his shaft. If you haven't added lube yet, now is a good time to add some.

6. **Fingers Up**: Use a light touch to gently run your fingers slowly from the base to just below the head. Try increased pressure. Try different speeds.

7. **Scrotum and Perineum Massage**: Gently run your hand down the penis base, over the scrotum, and massage the perineum. Some men prefer almost no touching there, some may be ticklish, and others thoroughly enjoy the feeling.

Taking the Hand-job to the Next Level: Now that the penis has been thoroughly massaged, move into the more erotic types of touch:

1. **Two Hand Squeeze**: Grab the penis with both hands and squeeze with one, then with the other. Alternate squeezing without moving the hands on the penis.

2. **Fists Sliding up the Shaft**: Grasping the penis firmly, start sliding one fist up the shaft, all the way over the head, then do the same with the other hand. Keep starting at the bottom and sliding up and over. Keep a steady speed but vary the pressure. Add a twist if you want.

3. **Fists Sliding Down the Shaft**: Again, use the hand over hand approach, but start at the head and slide down the shaft. Squeeze tightly so the penis has to force into the fist. This feeling of endless penetration into a tight, vaginal-like space feels amazing.

4. **Alternating 3 Up and 3 Down**: Use this double fisted approach for 3 up glides, then for 3 downward glides. Repeat, keeping the same speed but varying the pressure.

5. **Head and Frenulum massage**: grip the shaft firmly with one hand, then use the other thumb and fingers to tickle and massage the head and frenulum. He will feel a great contrast between the firm pressure on the shaft from the one hand and the soft strokes to the highly sensitive head and frenulum. Work around the head. Try some thumb circles on the frenulum.

6. **Single Hand Up and Down Cycles**: Grasp the shaft firmly and slowly move up to the head, then down to the base. Vary speed and pressure and try adding a twisting, corkscrew motion. Use both hands sometimes.

7. **Scrotum and Perineum Massage**: When he gets close to ejaculating (an 8 on the 10 scale), move back down to scrotum and perineum massage. Try splitting your fingers into a peace sign and massage with a finger on either side of the scrotum in a back and forth motion.

8. **Combos**: Massage the base of penis with one hand and the head with the other, or rub the perineum with one hand and corkscrew up and down the shaft with the other.

9. **Double-Hand Corkscrew**: You can finish a hand job in many ways, but if you want it to end in ejaculation, it's hard to beat the double hand corkscrew going from the head to the base. Again, grasp tight so it feels like he's entering a vagina, then twist down the shaft.

> Keep the same motion as he ejaculates. Unless he moves away, let those amazing feelings ramp down slowly instead of disappearing immediately after ejaculation.

You can add infinite variations to the above, but if you use these ideas you will give a world class hand job. I doubt most guys would have ever been that creative (or loving) to themselves. And that's the point, right?

Masturbation

While we're on the point, let's talk about self-gratification. Masturbation generally means pleasuring yourself using your hands. Almost everyone has done it—and probably felt guilty about it. Most of us probably caused our own first orgasm.

Do you remember yours? You should tell your spouse about it. Talking about sexual experiences helps unpack some of the weird emotional responses we tend to have about sex. I remember being a boy in the early stages of adolescence. I was asleep and dreaming about Sophia Loren. She was beautiful and exotic and voluptuous.

I woke up in a puddle of goo, wondering what in the world had just happened. We didn't talk about those kinds of things in my house, so I cleaned myself up and didn't ever tell anyone. Well, except for you.

Most folks masturbated (or had a wet dream like I did) to achieve their first orgasm. Masturbation can help you explore your sexuality and help you get to know your body better. Then you can lead your spouse to please you better.

On the other hand, you may masturbate as a stress reliever or just to have something to do. You may find you feel better if you have an orgasm every day or two and you can masturbate if your partner doesn't want to have that much sex. Or you may not have a partner. There are many different motivations for masturbation, but many Christians struggle with the morality of the act. Like other decisions involving sex, the Holy Spirit can give you direction here.

If when you read, "The Holy Spirit will lead you," you think, "I have no idea how that works," let me share an example. If you have a desire to masturbate, say a prayer and ask for God's direction. He cares about every sparrow and every hair on your head. He cares about this question too. You may get a strong feeling that it is fine for you to proceed. Or you may feel that you shouldn't. You may also not feel as though you receive an answer.

If you aren't sure, have a go at it. As we discussed in the last chapter, masturbation isn't a biblical sin. The "should I, shouldn't I" is a question of how you use your time. Well, it's more than that, but you have to determine the rest for yourself.

If you masturbate and feel guilty, explore that feeling. Pay attention to how you felt when you finished and how you feel the next day. Pray more and try to pay attention to the Holy Spirit's guidance.

You may decide that you should avoid masturbation. It will not be as good as being together with your spouse. Or you may find that it fills a void for you. Remember, things may also change in different phases of your life. Most of all, remember that it's great to be a Christian. God will lead us where he wants us to go, and it will be an amazing adventure!

Chapter 8

Sexual Epiphanies

We've examined life in Biblical times, the Song of Songs, and tried to understand challenging Bible texts. Now let's look at what it means to live as Christians today: what we believe about sex and how those beliefs might change. Let's start by talking about the life of a particularly despicable Christian: me.

Memories of a Christian Jerk

In the 1990s, Debby and I were cultural warriors against the "Homosexual Agenda."[132] She was on the board of Directors for an organization that provides Christian counseling for people who have same sex attractions. Teaming up with Exodus International, they tried to help folks change their sexual attraction. Spoiler Alert: virtually none of their clients experienced a change in sexual orientation.[133]

---

[132] Alan Sears and Craig Olsten, *The Homosexual Agenda: Exposing the Principal Threat to Religious Freedom Today* (Nashville, TN: B & H Publishing Group, 2003).

[133] Justin Lee, *Torn: Rescuing the Gospel from the Gays-vs.-Christians Debate* (New York, NY: Jericho Books, 2012), 87.

We also supported Alliance Defense Fund (ADF), which was founded by Evangelical leaders to promote religious liberty in America. In reality, though, ADF was a legal team that aggressively engaged its enemies: gay activists and the ACLU. We attended several ADF retreats for donors. It was, frankly, thrilling to be alongside these rich and successful Christians (they dwarfed us) to join in fighting for a Christian America. If God was with us, who could be against us?

Alan Sears was the leader at ADF and an expert in framing the battle as good vs evil. The Godly "Us" just wanted to continue our idyllic way of life while the despicable activists had a "Homosexual Agenda" that would destroy the American family. If we allowed the "Homosexual Agenda" to come about, we were told, America would lose God's special blessing.

Sears framed the arguments to vilify the leaders of the gay activist groups but portrayed gay people as poor souls trapped in a sinful way of life. In that way, we ADF supporters could feel good about ourselves for striving to help these poor sinners see the truth about their existence. All homosexuals needed to do was to repent and stop sinning.

I organized a fundraiser for ADF at the fanciest local restaurant. I pushed all my Christian friends to come and give money to the cause. When some wealthy friends showed little interest, I wondered how they could fail to support this important work. As an odd aside, our youngest daughter bussed tables at that restaurant. She later mentioned that a gay waiter had likely spit in our food. (Ah, the wages of sin...)

At that time, we didn't know any gay people and mostly spent time with other Christians. Then God started to tug on the rug under me. Debby and I met several men who identified as gay, and we liked them. They expected us to be jerks (since they knew we were Christians), but they liked us too. We felt God's love for one another.

My sense of rightness (which I now see as arrogant and self-righteous) began to deteriorate. I gained more friends who were part of the LGBTQ community and realized that none of them *chose* to be gay. None of them could *stop* being gay.

As I studied my trusty Bible, looking for direction, God broke me down with the following argument: If homosexual behavior was a sin, so was gluttony and greed.[134] Why were overweight people not

---

[134]Greed: **I Corinthians 6:10**: "Nor thieves, nor the greedy, nor drunkards, nor revilers, nor swindlers will inherit the kingdom of God." **Proverbs 15:27**: "Whoever is greedy for unjust gain troubles his own household, but he who hates bribes will live. **Psalms 37:21**: "The wicked borrows and does not pay back, but the righteous is generous and gives. **Titus 1:7**: "For an overseer (Elder of the church), as God's steward, must be above reproach. He must not be arrogant

persecuted by the church? Even if they prayed for forgiveness for overeating, they clearly continued in their sinful ways. Why were the rotund allowed to be pastors and teachers?

And consider greed. The greedy are celebrated. In most churches, a handful of financially successful folks run the show. If you've ever been involved in church leadership, you know the rich have loads of power. They may use that power with wisdom and humility (or not), but without them, many churches fail.

While it's possible to be rich without being greedy, that seems to be the exception and not the rule. It takes a concerted effort to amass money, and some amount of greed is present in that effort. If we define greed as an excessive desire for wealth, then most of

---

or quick-tempered or a drunkard or violent or greedy for gain.
Ephesians 4:18-19: "They are darkened in their understanding, alienated from the life of God because of the ignorance that is in them, due to their hardness of heart. They have become callous and have given themselves up to sensuality, greedy to practice every kind of impurity."
Gluttony: **James 5:5:** "You have lived on earth in luxury and self-indulgence. You have fattened yourselves in the day of slaughter.
Proverbs 23:20-21: "Do not be with heavy drinkers of wine, Or with gluttonous eaters of meat; For the heavy drinker and the glutton will come to poverty."

us who strive to gain wealth are occasionally excessive in our desires.

After experiencing this Gay, Glutton, or Greedy insight, I took several years to study the Bible. I focused on God's view of my G-cubed insight. My nightly research found no gay bias. Rather, I learned how much God hates pride and arrogance, which tend to be deep rooted and lead to cruelty.

My newfound thinking put me in good company. C. S. Lewis tackled this issue by pointing to Dante.[135] *The Inferno* lists pride, arrogance, and mean-spirited sins as the worst—deserving the lowest level of hell. On the other hand, Dante saw sexual lust as something more like incontinence—the least hateful of all sins.[136]

As I went through this study, Debby and I spent more time outside the bubble of church-friend relationships. We learned firsthand how unbelievers think Christians to be judgmental, hypocritical, anti-gay, and boring. Then they have little interest in learning more about Jesus. We found the lovely truth of Christ muddied by Christian intolerance.

---

[135] Dante was an amazing Christian writer of the 1300s. His masterpiece, *The Divine Comedy*, describes Hell (*Inferno*), Purgatory (*Purgatorio*), and Paradise (*Paradiso*). Comedy, in classical times, didn't mean lots of yucks. Rather it was the belief in an ordered universe set for our ultimate good.

[136] Janice Brown, *www.CSLewis.com,* The Official Website.

As Debby and I tried to live without superiority and judgement, our lives changed. We now have many non-Christian friends who are intrigued by our peace and joy. We get to be salt and light to wonderful people. [137] I think it makes God smile.

If this is God's truth for me, why are so many pastors, church leaders, and famous Christians anti-gay? Most were taught from the beginning that homosexuality is a sin. Since most of them aren't attracted to people of the same sex, it's easy for them to take the safe route and oppose homosexuality so as not to offend their constituents.

God often gives us the opportunity to be safe, popular, and wrong. He wants us to struggle toward the truth—to make courageous choices that honor him. Throughout history, God seems to have allowed his children to struggle with faith and obedience. As the old hymn says, "Trust and obey, for there's no other way to be happy in Jesus but to trust and obey."[138]

As I struggled to trust and obey, I changed from a comfortable, conservative Evangelical to a Christian who simply tries to follow God's direction each day. One of God's directions was to teach me that he loves homosexual people just as much as he does heterosexuals (and all the varieties in between).

---

[137] Matthew 5:13-16
[138] John Sammis, "Trust and Obey," 1887.

I began to learn how Evangelical Christianity affects kids who realize their sexual urgings aren't what heterosexual society would deem normal. These folks didn't decide to not be straight. Life would probably be so much easier for them if they could simply decide to be heterosexual. Science supports the theory that sexual orientation is largely dependent on a person's genetics. Many Christians question that science, but here's my biochemist son's take on that:

> When scientists hear people describe homosexuality as unnatural, it causes some head scratching because it's about as correct as the earth being flat—with just as much evidence.

> Homosexuality is so widely practiced in the animal kingdom that the scientist Petter Bøckman said, "No species has been found in which homosexual behaviour has not been shown to exist, with the exception of species that never have sex at all."

While I believe the science, compassion moved me more. Suicide is the second leading cause of death for teenagers.[139] Gay, lesbian, and bi-sexual teens are 4 times more likely to attempt suicide than their

---

[139] CDC, NCIPC. *Web-based Injury Statistics Query and Reporting System* (WISQARS), Online, www.cdc.gov/ncipc/wisqars.

straight peers.[140] A 10% uptick in suicide would be significant. 50% would be a crisis. This is 400%. It's staggering.

The suffering these teens must feel—willing to kill themselves for relief—should peg the compassion meter for Christ followers. If you have a sense that your child or some kid you know may be struggling with their sexual identity, please talk with them. Offer acceptance and love. [141]

If you think of homosexuals as enemies, you have a Jesus problem. He showed nothing but love for the people the rest of society shunned and degraded. His enemies were self-righteous religious jerks.

If you're a self-righteous religious jerk, be afraid. When Jesus said, "I never knew you," he was talking to religious people that fail to show love and forgiveness to the outcasts of society.[142]

On the other hand, you may want to love God and others, including gay people, but you aren't sure how to start growing in love for a group of people whose

---

[140] CDC, 2016, *Sexual Identity, Sex of Sexual Contacts, and Health-Risk Behaviors Among Students in Grades 9-12: Youth Risk Behavior Surveillance* (Atlanta: U.S. Department of Health and Human Services).

[141] https://www.believeoutloud.com/latest/christian-parents-gay-children or www.TheTrevorProject.org.

[142] Matthew 7:21-23

lifestyle and sexuality you don't understand. Start by learning.

LGBTQQIA

"LGBTQQIA" is the acronym of choice for people who identify as non-heterosexual. It is a better description than simply saying "gay people." So, what's it mean?

- **Lesbian**: a woman sexually attracted to women
- **Gay**: a man sexually attracted to men
- **Bi-sexual**: a man or woman sexually attracted to both sexes
- **Transgender**: a person who changes gender or gender identity
- **Queer**: an umbrella term for anyone not identifying as heterosexual
- **Questioning**: a person who is unsure about his or her sexual orientation or gender identity
- **Intersex**: a person whose gender is neither male nor female
- **Asexual**: a person who lacks (or has a low level) of sexual attraction

Jesus told his hearers (and the rest of us through the past 2000 years) to trust God and to love others. He often chastised the religious leaders to stop making rules for everyone. Jesus hated the rules and regulations and the resultant hypocrisy. Jesus loved God and he loved people—all people, LGBTQIA people included.

Consider this analogy: Jesus loved each of those people so much that when the grenade came into his barracks, he jumped on it. He sacrificed his life to save his buddies. I'm one of those guys who was standing around being a jerk when Jesus jumped on that grenade. I'm a life saved by Christ.

That's a pretty big burden to carry. Jesus sacrificed his life so that I could live. As I try to live a redeemed life, I struggle to hear the Holy Spirit's directions and to follow those directions in my relationships with all people.

Since I've come to recognize non-traditional sex as valid as my own weird variety, why did I populate the book with heterosexual instructions and examples? Because I need to write about what I know. Perhaps those with knowledge of non-heterosexual sex can add it to www.GreatSexChristianStyle.com.

Chapter 9

The Ins and Outs of Intercourse

Most books trying to improve your sex life go all KamaSutra when discussing intercourse, giving lots of positions for you to try. While I'm certainly a fan of weird positions, I take a different tactic in this chapter. *The Guide to Getting it On* has a chapter titled, "Intercourse: Horizontal Jogging," which provides lots of surprising information on copulation. [143]

The Insertion

Honesty time: many men struggle to get their penis smoothly inserted in the vagina. There are lots of things to bump up against down there that aren't the vagina—lots of missing going on. So it's not

---

[143] Paul Joannides, *Guide to Getting it On*. This book provides more useful detail than any other I've found. Though some may find the tone offensive and the nearly 1200 pages overwhelming, I highly recommend it if you want to learn more about sex.

necessarily a learning disability if the man still fumbles around down there after perhaps 5,000 lovemaking experiences with the same women...though in my case, it probably is.

Anyway, coming in at the wrong angle or poking the vaginal wall can be painful for the woman (men, think jab to testicles). Some women help glide the penis in for a smooth landing. I suppose if most men can't consistently hit the toilet bowl while urinating, it's no surprise we have a tendency to miss the vagina. If missing is an issue for you, talk about it, laugh about it, and keep trying. Even a blind hog roots up an acorn once in a while.

Now let's think about *when* to insert that penis in the passion process. There seems to be a natural tendency among men to want to get right to it. "I'm ready, she looks hot, let's go! And hey, what if that big asteroid hits the Earth in the next 30 seconds or I have a heart attack, or worse...the loss of an erection. Let's get this thing done!"

Fortunately, as Christian men, we know that resisting or, at the very least, being somewhat patient about our urges to do what comes natural is part of our spiritual growth. The "ground and pound" approach may work for monkeys and porn stars, but it's not what we're shooting for.

On the other hand, great sex doesn't come from following a bunch of rules. Great sex connects us physically, emotionally, and spiritually. It's a wonderful dance that varies all the time. Sometimes the penis can go in early and there's a beautiful closeness in simply rocking together. Other times lots of foreplay brings you both to the edge and intercourse is the grand finale, and a trillion other possibilities.

The only rule regarding penis insertion is don't shove into a dry vagina. Either wait for her natural lubrication system to kick in or use a lubricant. The natural lubrication system is different for every woman, so don't think of using lube as "cheating." You should always have a favorite lube nearby.

A surprising pattern having to do with insertion comes from an extensive sex survey.[144] Many women in the survey stated that their favorite part of intercourse was the penetration and first thrust. Men, discuss this with your lover and get into the specifics. Find out if she likes:

---

[144] *Guide to Getting it On,* 341.

1. a teasing series of short ins and outs, when you're barely inside the vagina;
2. a slow and steady push all the way in;
3. or perhaps she likes a big and hard pound from the beginning.

Her preference probably varies, but if she has a favorite, you should learn it and work it into the line-up. This is also a great opportunity for the woman to find what the man likes to feel upon insertion. Asking him to do what feels wonderful or pulling him in a certain way can increase your collective erotic experience.

Here's another vital piece of intelligence:

> Of the five thousand women who have taken our sex survey, the VAST majority either need finger stimulation on their clit or they grind their clitoris into the pubic bone of their partner in order to have orgasms during intercourse. Few have orgasms from thrusting alone.[145]

During intercourse, keep the clitoris in mind. Perhaps you will consider sliding your penis between the labia and rub the clitoris. She might really enjoy a

---

[145] *Guide to Getting it On*, 346.

gentle sliding motion. She can use her hand to rub it exactly where she wants to be rubbed, giving you some extra stimulation as well. Think of it like sliding a hot dog into a bun.

She could also squeeze her legs together to create more pressure, or she can spread her legs wide apart.

Since men often control the thrusting in intercourse, they have an opportunity to be creative and really pleasure their partners. Most men just pound away, wasting this occasion for distinction. Don't be that guy. Here are some thrusting options to try:

1. **Peek the Head Inside**: Use shallow and slow strokes. Pull out often and slide along the labia.

2. **Three Shorts and a Long One**: Go with three slow short strokes, then one luxurious long stroke. Then repeat. Pretend you are doing Morse Code and sending the letter V over and over. In fact, maybe learn all the letters and send her a message in code. (Hopefully that kind of advice reminds you this book was written by an engineer.)

3. **Five to Nine Shorts and a Long One**: If you want to go more old school, Tantric masters recommend between five and nine shallow

thrusts for every deep thrust. Perhaps bring the ratio down to 1:1 as arousal increases.[146]

4. **Variations**: Try hip swivels, side to side motions, and or simply rocking together.

5. **Public Bone**: The pubic bone rub creates some wonderful sensations. When the man is on top, he can move up a bit from his normal position and rub his pubic bone against her clitoris. Gently grind, pleasuring the clitoris while the penis fills the vagina. This is a great variation on the Missionary position.

6. **Angles**: If the above variations work well, see if any other penis angles provide extra pleasure for you and your lover. Gently experiment with different angles and see if you can find a winner.

7. **Understand the Cervix Bump**: When the penis hits her cervix, it can cause excruciating pain. If this is a problem, consider a penis ring (reducing depth of penetration) or positions that change the penis angle and penetration depth. Know that the cervix tends to rise a bit with arousal. Simply waiting for a beat upon entry before a deep thrust may solve the problem.[147]

---

[146] *Guide to Getting It On,* 348-349.
[147] *Guide to Getting It On,* 346.

Women can also take the lead in mattress dancing by being on top or by grabbing his hips while he is on top. The woman can perpetrate the items above and plenty more. Most men are thrilled when a woman demonstrates what she likes and wants in sex. Now let's consider some positions that work for both sexes.

Missionary Style

Think about intercourse positions, but let's start at a place no other book does. Does your prayer time include a period for praise and thanksgiving to God? Then the next time you pray, thank God for the Missionary position.

Think about how most mammals have sex. It's generally male behind female, "doggie style," which efficiently places the sperm deep in the vagina. But there is so much beauty in making love while facing your partner, looking into each other's eyes, kissing passionately, having full access to face, ears, chest, etc. We should praise God first for giving us our spouse and then for giving us this face-to-face missionary position in which to enjoy him or her.

Let's further explore the missionary position and some of its variations. Why is it called the "missionary position"? Alfred Kinsley first coined the phrase in his 1948 text, *Sexual Behavior in the Human Male*. He mistakenly thought missionaries in Polynesia taught their converts that this man on top position was the recommended way for Christians to make love.[148]

In the true story, the natives in that area made love using the doggy-style (like most mammals). They saw the white missionaries doing some horizontal dancing and thought it hilarious. Great conversation fodder around the campfire that night.

Can you imagine the teenage boys (because you know it had to be teenage boys) who peeked into the missionaries' tent that night? Looking, laughing hysterically with buddies, but still trying to be quiet? Some things never change.

The name stuck because folks tend to think of this position as tame or unexciting...as they imagined missionaries to be. I believe the opposite is true (about missionary position, not necessarily about missionaries), and here's why.

---

[148] Priest, Robert J, "Missionary Positions: Christian, Modernist, and Postmodernist," *Current Anthropology*, 42 (1): 29–68. From Wikipedia article on Missionary Position.

The substantial skin-to-skin, chest-to-chest, face-to-face contact provides for romantic coupling. Either partner can control the rhythm. Possible leg positions provide many different options.

Here are some missionary (or face-to-face) variations you may want to try:

a. **Basic Missionary**: Her legs outside his, with her knees bent and feet on the mattress, where she has the ability to move her hips and control the rhythm.

b. **Legs together Missionary:** Her legs together and his outside provides a tight squeeze on his penis. It's a surprisingly different feel.

c. **"V" is for Victory**: Her legs up on his shoulders provides a deep penis penetration and a different angle.

d. **Butterfly**: She can lie with her hips on the edge of the bed with legs on the floor and outside his. In this Butterfly position, the man stands (he doesn't have to support his weight on his arms) and it gives the woman more options for movement. While the clitoris isn't rubbed by intercourse in this variation, it is easily reached for manual stimulation.

e. **Standing Missionary**: While it looks good in the movies, and can be fun, it takes lots of fitness and energy. Also, most couple's genitals don't align when they stand, so you may need to do some shimming (pillows, an ottoman, this book...whatever works). By the way, do you know why Baptists don't have sex standing up? They're worried someone might see them and think they're dancing.

f. **Good Mornings**: This standing sex variation will work regardless of height differences, but requires some real effort from the man. As they face each other standing, she jumps into his arms and he leans down and forward, sliding penis into vagina. He will rock down to 90 degrees then back up to vertical. It's a workout.

g. **Face-to-Face in the Water**: this wonderful standing sex position uses the buoyancy of water to handle the gravity load. Face each other with knees bent in the water and rock back and forth. This position offers great clitoral rub on the pubic bone.

h. **Riding High**: One of the best secrets for wonderful missionary style sex is "Riding High." In most of the positions described above, the man can simply move up slightly from what feels natural and grind his pubic bone around the clitoris. This slight variation

       can substantially increase the woman's
       pleasure during intercourse.

i. **Pillow Support**: Another small variation that
       can make a big difference is adding a pillow
       or two under the woman's hips. The different
       angle can change everything. Make sure it is
       comfortable for her and does not cause back
       strain.

Far from unimaginative sex, you can spice up the missionary position with so many wonderful variations. Learn to have wild fun as you look into each other's eyes. Just remember that there is also a downside to missionary style. A man who tries to domineer and control his spouse may insist on using the missionary position because he can trap her with his weight and control the thrusting. If you only ever have sex in the missionary position and the man controls everything, you have a problem.

Cowgirl Position

Now let's consider the sex position in which the woman is on top and the man is on the bottom. It is often called the cowgirl position. The best part (and there are many) of this position is the amount of control the woman can have. She can decide penis angle, depth, frequency, and hip movement. Here are some things for cowgirls to consider:

Clitoral stimulation can be tailored to your exact desires. Lean forward and grind and gyrate against his pubic bone. By adjusting your hips, you can rub the penis right against your G spot. This will likely feel best when you are fully aroused, as the spot becomes more sensitive to pressure as more blood flows to the area.

Understand the powerful show you give in this position. As you arch your back, roll your head, and gyrate your hips, you turn on your lover. He can appreciate every expression on your face and full frontal nudity is always wonderful. You could also put on a camisole top or sexy bra for a teasing visual.

Here's a little secret you should know: most men love to watch a woman masturbate. The cowgirl position gives you the perfect opportunity to rub your clitoris (with fingers or a vibrating toy) while making love with him. Take charge. How would you like to have a simultaneous orgasm with your lover as you stared into each other's eyes? While that's plenty to shoot for, this would be the best position to accomplish that.

On the bottom, men should take the opportunity to learn. The way the woman moves and where she puts his penis in her vagina will provide great insight into what feels best for her. Since many women don't like to talk about these things, use the cowgirl position to learn what she has difficultly telling you.

Here are some cowgirl variations you may want to try:

a. **Basic Cowgirl**: The woman sits on top with her legs bent at the knees. This is the classic position where she can ride 'em hard and put 'em away wet.

b. **Laying Cowgirl**: She lies on top, with her legs either outside or inside his. He can hold his penis from this position and provide a direct clitoral penis rub while she controls the tempo.

c. **Lap Dance**: She can sit on his lap, facing him, on either a chair or bed. (Would you, could you in a chair? Would you, could you here or there? Would you, could you anywhere?)

d. **Reverse Cowgirl**: This position provides a delightful change of pace. The man will lay on his back and the woman will sit on him, facing his feet. In this position, the woman controls almost everything. Give yourself extra points for successfully swiveling from cowgirl to reverse cowgirl without disengaging the penis (or snapping it off)...which reminds me of one of my favorite lines: "I used to go out with a contortionist, until she broke it off."

e. **Corkscrew Cowgirl**: This is halfway between the cowgirl and the reverse cowgirl. In this variation, she can sit on top with one leg between and one leg outside his. Her options are many.

f. **Laid Back Reverse Cowgirl**: This is another variation of reverse cowgirl; she simply lies down from reverse cowgirl so her back is on his chest. Penile pop-out may be an issue in this position, but you won't know until you try.

g. **Better Than TV**: You have to try this one. Sit in a comfortable chair facing the TV (chairs that rock and swivel are ideal). I probably don't need to say this, but TURN OFF THE TV. The man will slump down in a comfortable sitting position and she will sit on his lap, facing him, with her legs on his shoulders or over the back of the chair. In this position, he gets to watch the best nature show ever. A vibrating toy may be added here with great results for everyone.

Just like in other positions, pillows can be a great addition for a cowgirl. Think of pillows as a secret weapon for better sex.

Doggy Style

Having covered missionary and cowgirl, let's get down and dirty to doggy style. There's something primal about this rear entry position. If it's good for the rest of the world's mammals, it may work for you.

The penis enters the vagina from the opposite direction of the missionary and cowgirl positions. You may be able to find great G spot stimulation in this angle. Here's a tip: the man should try swaying his hips instead of thrusting. Try to rub the penis head in small circles right at her G spot. Don't be a typical bonehead here: ask for directions! This rear entry position also gives the man a free hand for clitoral stimulation. He may want to stop thrusting, or even pull out for a bit, when she gets close to orgasm. This is a great position for simultaneous orgasming.

Women may feel that they have less control in doggie style, but her control just comes in a slightly different form. If she wants deeper penis penetration, she can arch her back upward, lower her chest, and spread her legs wider. On the other hand, she can go shallower by pulling her hips down. Explore these options to see if you can find a wonderful stimulation.

A word of warning for the male of the species: since this position can produce deep penis entry at a different angle, be gentle on that first long push. Mashing into her cervix is as bad as her hitting you in the testicles. If she indicates any pain, don't take it as a compliment on your amazing "hugeness." Instead, follow one of the most important (and ignored) rules of Christianity: Don't be a Jerk.

Here are some doggie style variations you may want to try:

1. **Basic Doggy**: She is on all fours and he mounts her from the rear. This can occur on the floor or on a bed. I suppose it could be performed while riding down a zip line, though the attendants would have to help you hook up the safety lines appropriately.

2. **Upright Doggy**: She's on her knees with torso upright and he's on his knees behind her. In this position, she can twist around and kiss her partner. You can also push up against a sofa backrest or a wall for a different feel.

3. **Corkscrew Doggy**: She kneels facing a couch and puts one leg up on the couch; he has one knee on the ground and the other under her knee on the couch. This position provides really deep penis penetration, so to paraphrase Sergeant Phil Esterhaus from Hill Street Blues, "Be careful in there."

4. **Laying Doggy**: This position has lots of options. During or after a back massage, he can slide in while kneeling behind her while she lies face down. You can also use a bunch of pillows to build some marvelous bridges. Vary the pillow orientation so the penis rubs against different vaginal locations (G spot lookout).

5. **Standing Doggy**: Like most standing sex positions, this one requires that you two are just the right height. In this position, the man doesn't have to lean, so he has both hands available to put to good use.

6. **Dog in the Water**: If you have an Endless Pool, this is a marvelous doggy style

variation to try. She will hold on to the bar and lean in to the current generator while he goes behind her. As the current rushes over her entire body, he can penetrate and rub her clitoris. Her legs can rest on the ground between his or float outside of his. This is a great position...you may want to purchase an Endless Pool just to try it. Though the dealer frowned upon trying this in their showroom.

Spooning

Let's move on to the final major category of intercourse. Spooning is similar to doggy style with both partners facing the same direction, the man behind, but it's so different. The bucking and wildness of doggy style contrasts the gentleness and romance of spooning.

From a purely physical viewpoint, spooning requires the least energy of any love making position. No one has to support their weight on their arms or even hold themselves upright. Spooning is a relaxed. You can lay side by side while gently thrusting and rubbing.

Here are a few advantages of spooning:

1. This provides the best clitoris access for the man of any position. He can rest his hand on

her body and rub for a long time without getting a sore wrist. She can guide his hand with her own to give him a bit of training. You can also easily apply lube from this position.

2. There is also great skin to skin touching. Legs can go in several different ways to change the contact and the penetration.

3. If either partner has concerns with how their body looks (and who doesn't?), spooning tends to minimize those concerns. Also a great position for sex during pregnancy.

4. Penis penetration depth tends to be more shallow in this position, which can sometimes be a plus.

5. She can squeeze her legs together for increased penis/vaginal pressure, or he can slide down and change the angle of entry.

6. If you decide you want to transition from a lazy lover position into a rutting dog, you can do so without missing a thrust.

Here are a few spooning positions you may want to try:

1. **Basic Spooning**: Fit yourselves together like spoons in a drawer. Lay on your sides facing the same direction with him behind.

2. **"T" Spoon**: Start from the basic spooning position. The man will then slide down and adjust to be more perpendicular to her. The angle and depth of penis penetration changes and the opportunities for clitoral stimulation are still good, but the skin to skin contact decreases in this variation.

3. **"Z" Spoon**: Start from the basic spooning position, then have her curl her knees up to her chest while he follows suit. He may want to adjust downwards a bit to improve the penis angle.

4. **Wide Leg Spoon**: She spreads her legs wide and over on the bed, opening up the vulva area for manual attention.

5. **Up Leg Spoon**: She spreads her legs by lifting one up in the air. A gentleman helps support the raised leg in this position while gently thrusting.

Spooning provides a great way for lovers to connect when their energy levels are on the lower side. Don't underestimate this position, though, as some wonderful orgasms can come from spooning.

Anal

The reason I'm sure God wasn't a civil engineer is that he ran a sewer line right through the middle of a recreational zone. What was he thinking? Well, some folks assume that septic discharging anus pipe should maybe have some in flow as well.

Like every other sexual decision, what you do with Uranus is between you and your spouse. Here are a few pointers to keep in mind, though:

1. If this is new to you, **start gently with fingerplay**. Use lots of lube and only go around the edges or maybe in up to one finger joint. The anus has a different elasticity than the vagina and doesn't stretch and lubricate nearly as well.

2. Since the anus is full of nerve endings (hemorrhoid sufferers can attest), some folks love some **finger play around the anus near orgasm time.**

3. Even though long term spouses probably share similar gut bacteria, fecal matter transfer can still cause some nasty prostate, urinary tract or other type infections. **A**

condom should always be worn for anal intercourse.[149]

4. If you are going to have anal intercourse, **use lots of lube and go very slow in and out.** Also, be careful how far the penis goes in. Again, the anus operates much differently than the vagina. If you're poking around down there, be gentle, and ask for lots of feedback.

5. Conventional wisdom tells the woman to relax if she's going to be receiving a penis up her backside. **If your husband pushes you for anal intercourse and you're hesitant,** I'd suggest you try a his-penis-sized dildo up the man's backside first so he can show you how to relax. Avoid sticking carrots or cucumbers up there as they may break off, then you've got some ER "splaining" to do.

6. Since the sphincter muscles excel at squeezing closed and capturing things, **be careful not to lose any toys up there.** Again, the ER trip just isn't worth it.

---

[149] *Guide to Getting It On,* 373-4.

Intercourse Frequency

A few years ago, I was teaching an adult Sunday School class and asked folks to raise their hands to indicate their normal frequency of sex. I told them the options would be:

1. Every day or two
2. Two or three times a week
3. Weekly
4. Monthly
5. Less often than monthly

I still remember the shocked look on their faces as I explained the survey. Then I watched those faces burst into laughter when I reminded them that the date on this fine Sunday morning was April 1st.

So how often do you have sex? Do you worry it's more (or less) than normal? That isn't an easy question for many couples. If the frequency of sex plagues your marriage, consider the concept of "the power of less desire." The person who wants less sex has a stronger negotiating position. The person requesting sex spends some of his or her relationship capital in the request. The less enthusiastic spouse has several options in response:

1. Deny the request

2. Postpone the request
3. Agree to participate with little effort
4. Agree to participate and try to find enthusiasm in the process

Each one of these is or can be a valid response. As you and your spouse work through these struggles, remember to love and forgive each other as best you can.

You shouldn't look to what works for others as the deciding factor for what will work for you and your spouse. You could have sex twice a day or twice a decade and still be at the right frequency for your relationship. Strive to find the intercourse rate that you both can be happy with.

Let's end this chapter by thinking about what makes intercourse great. If your answer is simultaneous orgasms, you're probably not going to feel successful most of the time. Take it down a level; there's a natural tendency to think intercourse a success if both parties orgasm, but there is usually more pride than love in that definition. I challenge you to let go of that orgasm attachment.

If you define success not in orgasms but in serving and loving each other, you will grow better in your relationship with God and each other. That's the real point of this mystery we call life.

Chapter 10

Romance: A Life Well Lived

Think about the last time you and your spouse had sex. How have you treated each other since? Did you affirm, build up, and act in a loving way, or were you selfish and lazy?

God designed you to live with integrity, courage, honor, joy, and kindness. If you strive to live that way, you will be romantic. Think about it. You love the person you're with. Be trustworthy. Be thoughtful. Be silly. Show the love.

God delights in you when you live this way with him and with our spouse. When you improve your relationship with God, your spousal relationship also improves, and vice versa. Work on one relationship is work on the other.

Think of foreplay as everything that has happened between you and your spouse from the last time you had sex. Strive to always be in a time of sex or romance. Sleeping in bed next to each other and reaching over to touch your spouse when you wake for a moment can be a gentle romantic element of living foreplay. All the little interactions that build love also build romance.

Even when tough times come, being conscious of our attitude can help grow our romantic relationship. Our 30-year-old daughter told her a boyfriend, "You know; I am a really difficult girlfriend."

He said, "No you're not."

"Yes I am," she said. "You don't know."

He said, "I do know. I'm just going to find you charming."

When I heard that story, I realized that I almost always find Debby charming, even when I'm mad at her, and she almost always respects me even when I act dopey. In the end, we all want to know we are loved and respected.

Don't Be a Jerk

So how do you build your relationship with your spouse? Start by not being a jerk. A jerk is selfish; he or she wants his or her own way and doesn't care about the desires of others. As children, we are naturally selfish. We mature into giving and loving people, but the inner jerk remains in all of us. We need to fight our entire lives against our inner jerk.

Romantic gestures, like sending flowers or giving a compliment, do *not* counteract day-to-day jerkiness. Think of your relationship like a bank account. Every jerk activity withdraws capital. Every kind, loving, Fruit of the Spirit activity deposits capital. To have a strong relationship, you need to be conscious of that ledger.

Agape Love

You know about Agape love. Christ modeled the unconditional, generous, and kind love that no one deserves but everyone enjoys. In order to build and strengthen your relationship with your spouse, strive for agape love. Work to build it as often as you can.

Remember that agape love doesn't take two. You can decide to love your spouse unconditionally and intensely, regardless of his or her behavior. You can love through anything if you choose to. But remember, don't use agape love as a strategy to change your spouse's behavior. If you do that, it's not agape love; it's manipulation behind a Christian mask. Don't do that.

Do you really believe Christ loves and accepts you, completely and unconditionally? Do you understand that nothing you do could make Christ love you any more or any less? The more you can believe that truth, the more you can live joyfully in the moment.

Believing in Christ's Agape love helps us let go of worries about the past or future, and as we more fully accept God's Agape love, we learn to love our spouse, our kids, our friends, and maybe even some of our enemies. As far as I can tell, that's why we're on this spinning rock.

Be Creative

Since I'm a planner, I often show my love to Debby by planning surprise vacations. It was sometimes just a quick overnight trip to a spa hotel or maybe a few days in the Caribbean. After her brother died in an accident, I took her on a surprise trip to Paris in attempt to ease her sadness. She didn't find out where we were going until the airport security agent told her. Being creative with grand acts of love is one way I work to build my relationship with Debby.

You don't have to copy what I did (though I am showing off a little). I want to encourage you to figure out what you could do to show your own unique love to your spouse in a creative and fun way. It starts with caring enough to make an effort. Remember, the opposite of love isn't hate; it's indifference.

Take time to think about what you love to do. Then think about what your spouse loves to do. Pray on it and God will lead you toward ways to show your love to your spouse.

One of God's attributes is creativity. He made us in his image, so don't try to claim you aren't creative. You may be afraid of looking stupid; that's not being uncreative, that's being prideful. That's the big sin to avoid. Making some mistakes while having fun seems more acceptable to God than sitting sour-faced and judging everyone else's fun.[150]

Your life may have a routine, but it doesn't need to be boring. Do some crazy stuff. Have fun. Get out of your comfort zone. Try new things and work to build up your marriage relationship.

Choose Your Response

If you aren't in love with your spouse, you're missing lots of joy. The thrill of romantic love brings out the best in us. It helps us become who we're capable of being.

But sometimes I'm in a crabby or judgmental mood and wonder why I don't have a spouse who treats me the way I deserve (which makes God either laugh or wince). Then I need to come up with strategies to change my stinking thinking.

---

[150] Luke 6:37-42 and John 8:1-8

For example,

1. **Strive to understand that we get to choose how we respond.** If you haven't read *Man's Search for Meaning* lately, please do. [151] It will get your mind right.

2. **Remember your history**. Remember how you fell in love. Recall the details and feelings you experienced. Let those history lessons inspire you to see your spouse with the old adoration.

3. **Understand that your current struggle can make your marriage stronger.** View it as a test to pass rather than a punishment to endure.

Make the choice every day to love and respect your spouse, no matter the situation.

Don't Badmouth Your Spouse, Ever

Don't speak badly about your spouse. Off-handed remarks you make to others in attempt to be funny are often hurtful. Try to avoid even thinking badly about your spouse. What's going on in your head will come out in your attitude, even if you don't say the words. Remember most human communication is in body language and tone of voice, not actual spoken words.

---

[151] Victor Frankl, *Man's Search for Meaning* (Boston, MA, Beacon Press, 1992).

Don't let others (friends, siblings, parents) speak badly about your spouse either; don't let them make you the martyr and your spouse the jerk. Be more courteous to your spouse than to any other human. Those little acts of kindness build substantial trust. The comfortable familiarity that follows is a great asset to your partnership. Protect it and expand upon it.

Lose Your Entitlements and Attachments

Nagging kills romance, so don't do it. Learn to accept more and live more in the moment. Don't get stuck in that unholy place of thinking you deserve better than what you have. If you're honest with yourself, you'll realize you are way more blessed than you deserve.

When that entitled feeling creeps into your mind, take a moment to think. Ask yourself, "Why do I feel like I deserve more?" Sometimes you'll conclude that you are upset about how your spouse behaved in a particular situation. Other times, though, you'll run right into unrealistic expectations. Name those entitlements so you can defeat them. The same goes for the attachment to the need to get your own way.

As we let go of our entitlements and attachments, we make ourselves more loving and lovable. Strive to become the best friend of your lover. What a powerful combination that can be! Think about whether or not you and your spouse are good friends.

If you aren't, why not? What do you need to accept and what do you need to change in yourself in order to become better friends? Work on the things that keep you from being good friends.

Don't settle for less with your spouse. Don't be content with simply staying married. Shoot for thrilling, romantic love. Nobody has it all the time, but strive for it always.

When the Baggage Comes Undone

We all bring childhood or early life difficulties into our marriages. Recognizing the deep love your spouse has for you can go far in helping us resolve those struggles. On the other hand, we may get to a place in which our past traumas become overwhelming or terrifying.

Don't expect your spouse to fix your past problems and issues for you. Seek professional counseling if you think it could help. View it as an investment in yourself and your marriage. Strive to understand and then move on.

If your spouse is struggling with past trauma, do what you can to support your spouse, but don't try to take on the burden for your spouse. Encourage him or her to seek professional help and offer to participate if your presence would fortify him or her in that situation.

Working on your own issues with the support of your spouse can build and enhance your relationship.

When You Can't Compromise

As we strive to live and exemplify the Fruits of the Spirit, we become more generous to one another. This often means making compromises, but there are times when meeting halfway doesn't work. We can't have half a child or buy one and a half a car (well, maybe if the one's a Mini-Cooper).

When compromise is impossible, we get the chance to live in the spirit of generosity. One of us will be happier than the other once the conflict is resolved. The happier partner should appreciate the gift and remember to live into the spirit of generosity in other uncompromising situations.

Tame the Tongue

Solomon warns us in Proverbs about the power of our words.[152] James makes it clear as well, and so does Jesus.[153] It comes down to a simple rule: "Don't say that mean thing that every part of you wants to say, even if you believe with your entire being that what you want to say is true."

---

[152] Proverbs 21:23, Proverbs 15:1, Proverbs 12:18, Proverbs 18:21, Proverbs 15:4, Proverbs 10:19, and so many more.
[153] James 3:2-10 and James 1:26; Matthew 12:33-37

If I want to say something critical, I don't. If I've thought about the issue in depth and really don't want to say the critical thing, then maybe I should, but even then, I try to avoid saying it. I don't need to say it if I know, deep down, my spouse already knows it. Criticism kills intimacy. Recognize the power of your words and avoid criticizing whenever you can.

Learn the Love Languages

Do you ever think about all the ways you can show your love to your spouse? In his book, *The Five Love Languages*, Gary Chapman examines that concept and illustrates five different ways to show your love:

- Words of Affirmation
- Quality Time
- Gifts
- Acts of Service
- Physical Touch[154]

When we learn our Love Languages, we gain a useful tool for understanding ourselves and others.

Gary Chapman spent years working with couples who were trying to save or improve their marriages. As he struggled to help, he discovered, again and again, the deep emotional need for love we all have.

---

[154] Gary Chapman, *The Five Love Languages* (Chicago: Northfield Pub., 2010).

As couples shared their secret pain, he would hear things like, "Our love is gone; our relationship is dead," and "We used to feel close, but not now," and "We no longer enjoy being with each other," and "We don't meet each other's needs." Husbands and wives had often tried to meet each other's emotional needs, but they were not very successful. It sometimes seemed as though one spouse spoke Greek and the other spoke Russian.

Chapman then developed the concept of the five Love Languages. Stated simply, most of us tend to show our love and seek love in one or more of the five ways listed above. One of those ways will be most significant to us—our primary Love Language. Our most intimate relationships (with our spouse, parents, children, close friends, etc.) will be greatly improved if we understand our own and our loved one's primary love language.

A person whose primary love language is *Words of Affirmation* seeks verbal affirmation. They need to be told they are appreciated. They need to hear things like, "Thanks for cleaning up the dinner dishes," or "I really am glad you took the time to come to my ball game." Complimentary, kind, and loving words matter to a person whose primary Love Language is *Words of Affirmation*. These words really register and make an impact. Conversely, someone whose lowest Love Language is *Words of Affirmation* will often disregard such statements or assume the words are said in order to manipulate them. As you can imagine, saying hurtful things to *Words of Affirmation* people hurts them more than you can imagine.

Quality Time is the primary Love Language of those who measure love in time spent. A person whose primary Love Language is *Quality Time* simply needs to spend good, focused time with the people they love. The cry for help from these people will sound like, "We never do anything together," or "You are always too busy with the kids (or your work) to pay attention to me." A *Quality Time* person will appreciate a date night sitting together in front of the fireplace. On the other hand, someone for whom *Quality Time* is their lowest Love Language will think of such an evening as, "Well we didn't really do anything; we just sat around."

We all know someone who has giving and receiving *Gifts* as their primary Love Language. These people are the ones who show up with a present and never miss a gift-giving opportunity. The person with *Gifts* as their primary Love Language feels special when he or she gives or receives gifts. It is not the size of the gift that matters; the sentiment behind the gift illustrates the love. A person for whom *Gifts* is the lowest Love Language tends to see gifts as manipulation.

The Love Language of *Acts of Service* involves doing things for others. Washing the dishes, changing the baby's diaper or a burned out light bulb, mowing the lawn, or making a special meal are all examples of *Acts of Service*. Someone with this primary Love Language, feels truly loved when his or her spouse puts forth the effort to perform helpful tasks. On the other hand, a person for whom *Acts of Service* is the lowest Love Language may tend to see all that activity as avoidance of the real issues.

Having *Physical Touch* as your main Love Language means you desire physical contact with a loved one. A *Physical Touch* person will value holding hands, hugs, playful punches on the arm, and other physical contact. A handshake is significant to this person, as is sexual intercourse (an amped up version of the handshake?). A *Physical Touch* person will place high value on any type of touch and physical contact. Those for whom *Physical Touch* as one of their lowest Love Languages tend to see physical contact as insignificant. A *Physical Touch* person who has suffered past abuse or rape will struggle to trust anyone due to this heightened violation. As I stated before, a skilled counselor can help here.

To illustrate the usefulness of knowing your Love Language, imagine a husband (Bill) and wife (Naomi) who are struggling in their marriage. Bill feels like he puts forth the bulk of the effort to keep the marriage going and resents Naomi for not trying harder. Naomi also believes she puts most of the energy into their relationship and is angry at Bill for not noticing. Bill works all day at a telephone company and then comes home to mow the lawn, pull weeds, pick up the kids' toys, do the laundry, wash the dishes, and coach a softball team. At the end of one of these busy days, when he feels a little frisky, Naomi rebuffs his romantic advances. Bill lies in bed and seethes, wondering why Naomi appreciates him so little and has become such a selfish witch (or sentiments to that effect).

Naomi, on the other hand, stays home with the three children in the mornings and works as a waitress during lunch and dinner. She tries to be a good mother by reading to each child and spending time with them; she does the bulk of the housework and she waitresses to bring in extra money. Naomi enjoys the waitressing because her regular customers tell her how wonderful she is, which she rarely hears at home any more. She falls into bed at night, physically and emotionally exhausted, and then Bill pouts when she does not feel like having sex. She wonders how she married such an insensitive dolt.

Do you see the Love Language clues in this scenario? They are right out there in the open, just as they are in most relationships. Bill's primary Love Language is *Acts of Service* with *Physical Touch* a close second. *Gifts* is in third place, while *Words of Affirmation* and *Quality Time* are last. Bill does things other women complain their husbands never do. Bill feels that he puts forth so much effort and is not appreciated by Naomi, and he feels particularly upset about this issue at bedtime.

Naomi's primary Love Languages are *Quality Time* and *Words of Affirmation*. *Physical Touch*, *Acts of Service*, and *Gifts* are not especially important to Naomi. When Bill comes home from work and rushes right out to mow the lawn or throws in a load of laundry, Naomi wishes he would just sit down with her and talk about the day. Naomi knows she should appreciate all the work Bill does, but instead she finds herself resenting the work and Bill. Then she feels guilty. She knows they are growing apart, and it scares her.

Like many married couples, Bill and Naomi have different Love Languages. If they don't address the issue, they will probably continue to drift apart. Perhaps Bill will find temporary comfort in the arms of a co-worker or a softball team mom, and their marriage will go down in flames. Perhaps nothing dramatic will happen, but their sense of love and closeness will just fizzle away to nothing. However, Bill and Naomi could decide to take action and turn their marriage around.

When Bill realizes that time and encouraging words truly matter to Naomi, he will begin to see that sitting and talking with her or giving her a compliment is an act of service and not as a waste of precious time. These efforts on Bill's part will be emotionally rewarding for both of them. Naomi will hear the Love Language she understands, and Bill will see the effort as an act of service, a Love Language he relates to.

Naomi will strive to do little extra things for Bill that she knows he appreciates. She may still get more compliments as a waitress than she gets at home, but she knows Bill is trying, and that helps her feel loved. Their love-making will improve as their love grows and this aspect of their marriage will motivate Bill more than Naomi can ever imagine. Understanding and using the Love Language concept can help produce strong, happy, enduring relationships.

In reviewing this concept, our niece Wendy became intrigued with the Love Languages and decided to try it. Her husband had a week of vacation during which he planned to get some things done around their house. Wendy correctly guessed that *Words of Affirmation* was her husband's primary Love Language, though they were not that important to her. Wendy spoke encouraging words to Steve each day when opportunities presented themselves.

After only a few days, Steve told her how much he appreciated Wendy's encouraging words. As a couple, they had nourished their love. A strong marriage just grew a little stronger.

If you want to learn to use the love languages, sit down with the list above and think about what your own Love Languages might be. Write them in order and do the same for your spouse. Try listing the Love Languages of a few other folks as well—kids, parents, siblings, etc. Keep that list. Over the next few days, try to see those people through the lens of Love Languages. Learn to spot instances of high value and low value Love Languages. Try to put this knowledge into action. Keep trying.

Use the Love Languages to continue growing in your marriage.

Chapter 11
Toys, Stories & Games

Buzzzzz. Buzzzzzzz. Buzzzzzz. That's what our daughter heard from passing kids as she walked down the hallway of her high school. Debby and I had gone away for a weekend. Teenagers were in our house—in our bedroom, in fact. They looked under the bed and found the stash of vibrating sex toys I store in an old ammunition case (seems appropriate right?).

The school kids thought it hilarious that we old folks had vibrating sex toys. Let's look into why you might also find it hilarious and want some for yourself.

Toys that Go Bump in the Night

I don't want to put too fine a point on it, but the gentle little vibrating sex toys are female orgasm magic. And they aren't bad for men either. The vibrations create sensations unlike anything else, and I'm not the only one who thinks so.

About half the men and women in America have used vibrators for sex.[155] But for some reason, people who regularly attend religious services are less likely to have felt the vibe.[156] I'm here to change that.

Vibrators have become so mainstream that Wal-Mart, common drug stores (such as Walgreens), and even some convenience stores ("I'll have a super Slushie and an orgasm maker") now sell vibrators. Sites like ComeAsYouAre.com or MyPleasure.com sell every available sex toy. Trust me, you will be overwhelmed with options.

Allow me to guide you. Let's start at the beginning and assume you have never used a sex toy. Let's ignore butt plugs and dildos and all other implements of destruction for the moment and focus on vibrators.

Think about how you might use a vibrator. You won't find an instruction manual in your vibrator package, so I'll share some tips. Don't start by shoving the vibrating piece of plastic into one of your body cavities. Start with external use, and have some lube handy.

---

[155] Two new national surveys from Indiana University recently published in The Journal of Sexual Medicine, NYT 6/26/09
[156] Herbenick, D., Reece, M., Sanders, S.A., et. al. "Prevalence and Characteristics of Vibrator Use by Women in the United States: Results from a Nationally Representative Study," in *Journal of Sexual Medicine Early View,* June 2009.

Get comfortable running the device on your hands, feet, legs, and belly. If there are variable vibration settings, get a sense of how it feels on each of them. Take some time exploring the sensations it produces on the rest of your body before you move to your erotic zones.

See what you like and don't like. Think about what your partner may enjoy. Here are some tips:

1. **Use the different surfaces of the vibrator**. Each surface will provide a unique sensation.
2. **Vary the pressure.** Try a light and gentle touch and then a firm one, pressing against the skin.
3. **Play with the different speed and pulsation settings.**

Understand that vibrators can take you to orgasm quickly, which is why they are so popular. But what's the fun in rushing to orgasm? Try using these little wonders to take you to the edge, but then back off. After you try that a few times, finish and you'll find the orgasm is intense.

Now that you have an idea of how you'd use a vibrator, think about how to purchase one. You can search "vibrating sex toys" on Amazon and see lots of options. Or go to ComeAsYouAre.com or MyPleasure.com and see many more. They ship in non-descript packaging and charge the credit card with a name that doesn't scream sex toy. You could also go to a Babeland store and shop with cash in person.

Regardless of where you shop, here are some options to consider:

1. **Power Source**: We've already begun by narrowing it down to a vibrator for external use. The next consideration is power source:
    a. Battery operated vibrators tend to be the lowest cost and least powerful vibrations. They tend to break. The more expensive ones seem to be better made and last longer.
    b. Plug-ins cost more and can be more powerful but have a wire that can get in the way during lovemaking.
    c. Rechargeable batteries tend to cost the most, but they have powerful batteries for a good buzz and no power cord to get in the way.
2. **Vibration options**:
    a. A simple on or off option is sometimes nice.
    b. Varying the intensity of the vibration movement (from a gentle purr to a thumpity-thump) changes the experience.

    c. Varying the type of vibration from pulsating to escalating to all kinds of other patterns may also work for you.

3. **Noise**: Some are quiet and some aren't. If this matters to you ("Mommy, what's that funny noise and why are you and Daddy wrestling?"), then have a listen prior to purchase.

4. **Material**:

    a. Hard plastic (acrylic) materials are often used for external use. These are easy to clean and rarely cause allergic reactions.

    b. Soft plastics used for internal use sometimes cause allergic reactions. Silicon tends to be hypoallergenic, but it is expensive. Cheaper versions that claim to be made of silicon may not be.

    c. Avoid the potentially toxic phthalates (pronounced "tha-lates"), which are used to help to soften the toys. If it has a strong chemical smell and is clear and cheap, don't use it. Items labeled "100% Silicon" are a better option.

    d. If you are sensitive to multiple chemicals, you may struggle to find a material that doesn't cause a reaction. You may want to use a condom on the toy. If you have a latex allergy, use a non-latex condom.

In the end, just buy something and give it a whirl. See what you and your partner think. By the way, another added bonus: the vibrator can reduce your workload.

If you like your vibrator and decide to try some other sex toys, here's a list to help you with terminology and functions.

1. **Dildo**: a phallic shaped sex toy with no motors or moving parts. They are made of soft or hard plastic, glass, metal, wood, or organic material (think banana). Dildos come in all shapes and sizes. The Bible describes the use of a dildo, which means it was common enough for readers of that day to recognize.[157] Dildos get used for vaginal or anal penetration, either in masturbation or by a partner in love making. I'm guessing you knew that...

2. **Penis ring**: a flexible plastic, rubber, or leather device that encircles the penis (and possibly the scrotum) to restrict penis blood flow and keep harder and longer erections. The restrictive pressure can be pleasurable for the man. A vibrating feature can be added to stimulate the clitoris. Note to men: don't wear it too long or your penis may fall off. You think I'm kidding...

---

[157] Ezekiel 16:17.

3. **Anal beads**: a string of plastic spheres that can be pushed up the anus (with lots of lube), then pulled out slowly to stimulate the sphincter muscles. I hear if you can get the timing right, pulling these out at orgasm is wonderful good. But don't lose them up there. If you do, don't tell the person in the ER you sat on them by mistake. Learn to own your idiocy.

4. **Penis Sleeve**: a cylindrical sheath that the penis slides into for masturbation. Think faux vagina. The Fleshlight series of penis sleeves are probably the best selling sex toy line. On the other hand, you could save $85 and cut the end off of a banana, squeeze the banana out, fill it with hot water, and have at it.

5. **Butt Plug**: an anal dildo designed to stay in place during sex. They come in a variety of shapes but generally have a wider handle on the end to keep it from going all the way in. The glass and stainless steel models can be heated or cooled because who doesn't want a cold, steel cylinder shoved up their butt?

6. **Pumps**: a toy used to create a negative pressure (think vacuum) on nipples, the clitoris, or the penis. The pressure causes blood to flow to the area, enlarging the erectile tissue and increasing sensitivity. Products range from inexpensive plastic pumps to high tech ones with gauges. It's a two-part toy: a suction device against the skin

and a pump to create pressure. The suction device can be removed after a short time or kept on during love making. Some pumps are removable. I remember when we were first married Debby chased me around our room naked with the vacuum cleaner hose. Watching my penis disappear into that hose was a terrifying moment for me...Debby couldn't stop laughing.

Let's not limit our thinking about sex toys to the kind you can buy from the naughty store. You can also build your own. My favorite is double shower heads.

Taking a shower together brings up the age old struggle, "Who's going to be warm and comfy under the gentle spray and who's going to be cold?" A double shower head takes that question off the table but introduces some delightful new ones, especially if the one shower head is handheld with a 5' hose.

This type of shower is a good place to learn a few things about what feels good for your spouse. If you begin by washing each other and kissing with all the water spray, it can get quite erotic. Rather than finishing in your normal way, consider using the hand held shower to finish yourself while your spouse sits down and watches. It may make you a bit uncomfortable to masturbate in front of your partner, but it can be a freeing experience. Watching your partner masturbate should teach you a few things about what feels best for him or her.

You could also build a stripper pole, rings, or high hand holds to hang from. Other ideas are to build a hammock, a trapeze, or whatever else your crooked little heart desires. GreatSexChristianStyle.com has a list of inspirational movie scenes and some how-to instructions.

That should be all you ever wanted to know about sex toys and more. Perhaps you're now inspired to give a new toy a try. Now let's talk about stimulating your partner's brain for sex.

Erotic Stories

Getting yourself in the mood for sex can be enhanced through the use of erotic stories or visuals. You and your spouse might enjoy paging through Vogue magazine together, looking at the beautiful people wearing high fashion. Or perhaps you might like to read a titillating story to get your motor running. Sometimes the love scenes in a movie will put you in the mood. Even sharing a fantasy or recalling a sexy memory can do the trick.

I group all these sexual turn-ons under the label "stories." Pornography also falls into this category. But let's first address pornography as a separate item. While it's certainly arousing for most folks, it doesn't seem very God-honoring. I know, I know; it seems I've taken the libertine view on almost every sexual subject so why draw the line at porn? Here's why:

- The actors in the films seem fake—particularly all those pretend female orgasms.
- The films are made for camera angles; they don't illustrate the way real people have sex. Porn is terrible as an instructional video ("Let me pull my penis out of your butt and put it right in your mouth" isn't a good plan).
- Porn is like watching a baseball game with only third base and home plate. Real great sex spends lots of fun time on foreplay.
- Ejaculating on to your partner's face ("cream pies") is just rude.

Also, porn can become an addiction for many men. Loads of family misery can come from an addiction to pornography. Why take the risk when there are so many other great ways to get turned-on and enjoy sex with your partner?

Back to erotic stories: I made a list of ways to engage with erotic stories:

1. **Movies**: Watching a movie together can be a wonderful way to prepare for fun sex. Maybe a comedy will relax you. Maybe a

romance will do the trick. Here are some movies I recommend:

  a. The Well Diggers Daughter
  b. The African Queen
  c. Bread and Tulips
  d. It Happened One Night
  e. Populaire
  f. Bringing Up Baby
  g. To Rome with Love
  h. Some Like it Hot

2. **Erotic stories**: Reading erotica, either out loud to your partner or reading your own story to yourself, can be a turn on.

3. **Role playing**: Make up your own erotic stories and act them out together. Perhaps you're lying on a deserted beach in the Caribbean.

4. **Erotic images**: Looking at images together and talking about what you like can be sexy. Try getting frisky with Pinterest.

Remember to be cautious when making any foray into erotica. Try to walk that line between things that are sexy and things that are also God honoring. For example, reading a story about a spouse having an affair may be steamy, but it may motivate you in a direction you don't want to go. Lots of erotica is like that, so be careful to avoid it.

But you don't necessarily need to avoid all of it. Just be careful and selective. Some Christian erotica at GreatSexChristianStyle.com may work for you, but you or your spouse may find it offensive while I find it perfectly God-honoring. As for everything in life, listen for the Holy Spirit's guidance.

Games that End With a Bang

Imagine you and your spouse are planning an evening in which you will end up making love but neither of you feels very creative or high energy about it. This is a good time to consider sex games. The randomness of the game moves you into a new love-making pattern. Remember, innovation is one of the secrets to a lifetime of great sex with your spouse.

Consider Strip Blackjack, with each hand dealt, the loser removes a piece of clothing. Add a twist by making sex cards (back massage, head massage, foot massage, masturbate, oral, choice) to be used if a blackjack is dealt or after the loser is naked. Blackjack is fun because of the element of skill and risk/reward. Do I take the next card or do I hold?

Or try "Rock, Paper, Scissors" or "Go Fish" or any other game you know. Be creative and adapt something. You could make sexy croquette or racquetball or cricket. (Ok, maybe not cricket. I don't really know how you would adapt cricket into a sex game. If you figure it out, let me know.)

Another variation on the sex cards is to make two colors and have the winner pick one of each color.

1. **First color**: action.
   a. Suck
   b. Lick
   c. Blow
   d. Massage
   e. Kiss
   f. Nibble
2. **Second color**: location
   a. Face
   b. Privates
   c. Neck
   d. Feet
   e. Breasts
   f. Ears

At some point the game will end and you'll just keep picking cards and laughing at the combinations. Then it turns to something else entirely. Let that happen.

Hopefully this chapter made you ask the question, "Where do we draw the line in our sex life?" Here's my final piece of advice: Don't do anything that you wouldn't want to explain to the paramedics or the police.

Chapter 12

If I Were Raising Teenagers Again

Debby and I taught our kids they should abstain from sex until marriage and that marriage was to be a lifelong, monogamous, male-female relationship. But I guess we didn't because none of our kids believe that as adults. After much Bible study and prayer, Debby and I don't either.

I remember how angry our teenage daughter was when she found out Debby and I had not followed the abstinence course ourselves...not even remotely.

As a kid, I wasn't taught that sex should be reserved for marriage. It was the 1960s, and I don't think I'd ever even considered that concept. When Debby and I started dating at 17, we waited a few weeks to have sex because I'd read somewhere that it was better to get to know each other first. We were sexually active from 17 (we got married at 21) and I never felt ashamed or guilty of that fact.

In our mid 20s, we began attending the conservative church where Debby grew up. It was there that I first heard the teaching of abstinence. It made sense to me, and like many parents, I embraced the idea of helping my kids avoid unnecessary pain.

Our daughter became sexually active in her mid-teens, feeling a mixture of guilt and rebellion. Worse than that, though, she was unprepared to handle aggressive teenage boys and all the attention she was receiving from adult men. She engaged in many destructive teenage behaviors, which she's fortunate to have survived.

She's now a charming adult with a colorful history, but things could have been so much worse for her. If I was raising a teenager again, I'd do it differently. Here's what the Bible says, what the Church says, and what I'd do differently raising teenagers today.

What the Bible Says

The Bible stipulates in several places that women should be virgins at marriage.[158] It never mentions any similar requirement for men. This can't just be an oversight. God isn't knocking the heel of his hand

---

[158] Leviticus 21:13, Deuteronomy 22:20-22, Exodus 22:16-17

into his forehead and saying, "Oh man, I forgot to mention that men should be virgins at marriage too."

In previous chapters, we learned that the ancient culture required women to be sexually pure, both prior to and in marriage, so the lineage of the children would be uncontested. Men had no similar requirements. And since men tended to marry in their mid-20s, sex with slaves and prostitutes was a normal occurrence.

The Bible was written in that cultural context and didn't address the need for pre-marital purity for men. In fact, there is no Hebrew or Greek word for sex prior to marriage. In those times, marriage wasn't similar to what it is today. With women in a role like slaves, comparisons between Biblical marriage and our contemporary marriages almost don't make sense.

So how did we get the idea that the Bible requires sexual purity prior to marriage? The King James Version of the Bible often translates *pornea* as "fornication." People tend to define "fornication" as sex prior to marriage. Hence many pastors preach that the Bible prohibits sex prior to marriage.

Pornea seems best translated as "sexual sins," and those sins aren't clearly defined. I believe God intended his followers to consider the cultural context of the Bible at the time it was written and to consider the cultural context of the current times when interpreting its teachings. Through those two considerations, the Holy Spirit can give you guidance for how you should live.

Therefore, I don't see any strong Biblical commandment prohibiting sex before marriage. The Bible tells us often not to be sexually immoral but doesn't define what that means.[159] God seems to give us some grace here.

What the Church Says

The Church, historically and today, offers much less grace when it comes to rules of sex and marriage. The vast majority of churches teach that sex is allowable only between a man and woman in a Christian marriage. But if the Bible isn't clear about this, where did the idea come from?

The early Church cultivated a strong anti-sex viewpoint. Some leaders wrote that total sexual abstinence was required of all Christians. Others

---

[159] I Corinthians 6:12-13, I Corinthians 6:18, II Corinthians 12:21, Ephesians 5:3.

taught that sex was meant for procreation only. On a more positive side, the early Church also helped end the common practice of sex with early adolescent boys and girls (whether slaves or prostitutes). Christian men were also told to stop having sex with slaves and prostitutes, which was a radical idea at that time.

Church leadership, then as now, was a difficult job. Even if we try to strongly incline toward grace, an organization like a church can't be a "free for all." If the Pastor says he feels the Holy Spirit telling him to take in a concubine in addition to his wife, the church Elders will need to pass judgement on those shenanigans. Someone needs to decide who's allowed to teach the children and what to teach them. Christian congregations still exist that teach sex for procreation only—though there are very few as men tend to be pastors—and congregations also exist that share my freethinker views.

The vast span of beliefs held by Christian churches gives Christians an opportunity to worship in a place that shares their beliefs about sex. I don't imagine most folks spend much time struggling through why they believe what they believe about sex, but raising teenagers tends to get those questions frothing.

What Will You Say?

If you have kids nearing their teenage years, how well informed do you want them to be about the following?

1. The mechanics of sex and various types of sex
2. Pressures to be or not be sexual
3. Feelings, attitudes, and values about sex
4. Homo-erotic feelings, a lack of sexual feelings, etc.
5. Rape and abuse in all its ugly forms
6. Alcohol, drugs, and sex
7. Sexually transmitted diseases and levels of protection
8. Pregnancy prevention and levels of risk
9. Locations for sexual activity and the risks involved with particular locations
10. What consent means and how is it given throughout the process of sex

Think about all the teenagers who commit suicide, are raped, or become pregnant. Knowledge about sex will help your teen better navigate these risky years. This can't just be a one-time, "birds and bees" talk. It needs to involve years of increasingly detailed and specific discussions between parent and child.

Think about how you convey your love of God to your children. You don't tell them one time and then check it off your list. Hopefully your entire life models your love of God and you fill in the words as needed. God ordained sex as a beautiful way to procreate and to grow in love and enjoy each other. We need to teach that to our kids. The following dialog shows one way to cover the ten topics on the list:

Me: Let's take a few minutes and discuss sex again.

Teen Daughter: Ewwww. Let's not.

Dad: Oh, come on. This is important stuff, and what they teach in school doesn't cover it. When I started having sex, I thought the girl could only get pregnant during her period. We were so nervous and shy that we didn't talk about it. Looking back, I'm amazed she didn't get pregnant. Do you know how the baby making process works?

Teen Daughter: Yes, Dad.

Dad: Can you please explain it to me?

Teen Daughter: The girl's menstrual cycle runs for 28 days. She gets her period for about a week, then is most likely to get pregnant 14 days after the start of her period. Sperm and eggs can live a long time, so there really isn't a "safe" time.

Dad: Great. That was very clearly stated. You obviously understand the mechanics of sex. But there is so much more to sex than the mechanics...I think of the great joy in holding hands, walking and talking, to deep and passionate kissing to touching each other in pleasing ways. That's all way beyond the mechanics. Do you have any questions about any of that?

Teen Daughter: Well, this is embarrassing, but kids are always talking about oral sex and I don't exactly know what that means. I mean, I sort of do…

Dad: Sure. Your brother asked that same question. I mentioned earlier about part of sex being touching each other in pleasing ways. Well, the tongue and mouth can be a way to touch your partner. The basic definition of oral sex is the use of the tongue or mouth on the penis or the vulva. It can be enjoyable for both partners...

Teen Daughter (interrupting): Ok, great. Thanks. That's enough about that.

Dad: Let's talk a bit about the pressures to be or not be sexual. When you have feelings for a boy and it's mutual, there's a normal romantic sequence: talking, spending time together, holding hands, kissing, exploring each other's bodies, etc. That sequence can proceed over months or minutes. There are many kinds of pressure—from your partner or even from your own body—that can push it to happen quickly. You need to consider those pressures before they happen and try to be prepared.

Teen Daughter: Well, I don't think anyone I care about would push me to do anything I wasn't ready to do.

Dad: But that's where you're wrong. I'm not saying it's just boys that do this. The teen years are the natural time to break parental bonds and focus on yourself. It's normal. Then, add in all the pressures teens feel about sex: Why am I a virgin when I have friends that aren't? Is there something the matter with me? Am I normal? I wonder what it's like. Then, add the natural teen selfishness to all those sex anxieties and you get a high pressure situation...even if everyone involved is wonderful good folks.

Teen Daughter: Ok, I get that there's lots going on and it would be easy to feel or exert pressure. But what am I supposed to do about that?

Dad: The first thing is to know it's coming—to be prepared and not be bushwhacked by all those feelings. The best way to be prepared is to take time to think through your beliefs and attitudes about sex. Just like in your spiritual life, these will be your decisions, not Mom's and mine.

Teen Daughter: Well, I don't really know what I think.

Dad: That's to be expected, but it is a big deal, and you will be making the decisions. Read, talk with folks whose opinions you value, pray, and do anything else that makes sense to you.

Teen Daughter: Well, I have a friend who is a little worried because she wonders if she likes girls more than boys.

Dad: Lots of folks wonder about homoerotic feelings in their teen years. You may have these stirrings, and you aren't quite sure what they even are. It's all confusing. Or you may not feel those stirrings, and then you wonder what's wrong with you for not feeling what everyone else seems to be feeling. Try not to get too worried. Time will likely clear most of this up for you. You won't figure it all out immediately.[160]

Teen Daughter: Just wait...you're telling me to read and talk to people to figure out what I believe but also to just relax and not worry about it.

Dad: Yes.

Teen Daughter: That doesn't make sense.

Dad: Well, sex defies easy answers. My advice is to think and pray and learn what you can but also to relax and try not to worry too much about it. Worrying never helps. Being prepared helps, especially being prepared to say "No." Our culture discourages women to speak up for themselves. When things start to heat up, they can quickly progress further than you thought they would and are willing to go. The wise person prepares for that. Learn how to say no. Say it.

Teen Daughter: No.

---

[160]If the teen you are talking with seems to be truly struggling with same sex attraction, your answer needs to be different here. So many kids from Christian homes end up as runaways or suicides because they feel so judged about who they think they are. Add bullying of kids that seem different and you've got a toxic mix. Pray for love and discernment about how best to proceed if you think your teen may be on this path.

Dad: Really say it.

Teen Daughter: No.

Dad: C'mon, say it like you mean it!

Teen Daughter: NO!

Dad: That's the way! I know this is uncomfortable to discuss, but so many teens and pre-teens are sexually assaulted or raped. It happens to almost half of all girls and usually goes unreported. There are many forms of abuse: physical, sexual, financial, emotional...the list continues. And you need to learn how to combat that horror. Abusers will usually try to separate their victim from all other supportive relationships. The abuser will make the victim feel bad about herself or himself. Abusers use shame or guilt to get what they want. You should try to understand this process, both to help keep you out of abusive relationships and to look out for your friends who might be abused.

Teen Daughter: I do have a friend who is in a weird relationship right now. Her boyfriend gets so jealous and tries to control everything she does. He also says mean things to her.

Dad: Those are classic signs of the beginning of an abusive relationship. Is he older than her?

Teen Daughter: Yes, a couple of years older. You have to promise you won't tell her parents...one of the things she likes is that he gets alcohol for her.[161]

Dad: That highlights another important point about sex. Alcohol really loosens a person's inhibitions. It tends to provide a feeling of confidence. Many sexual encounters among teenagers simply wouldn't happen without alcohol. It's important you understand that alcohol or drugs change your decision-making abilities and process. Think morning after regrets.

Teen Daughter: I know I'll be nervous when the time comes for me to cross that line...whenever that is.

---

[161] One of the lack of actions I most regret in my life happened in a conversation similar to this. My 14-year-old daughter told me about a friend who was developing a close relationship with her middle school teacher. It just felt to me that it could lead to abuse. My daughter was adamant that her friend told her in confidence and that I couldn't tell her parents or approach the teacher. It did turn into sexual abuse (for which the teacher is now in jail) but looking back I should have ignored confidentiality when potential abuse was possible. I pass this along to encourage you to protect the little ones.

Dad: Yeah. My hope is that you think through your beliefs and desires and make your decisions based on those, not on a random high from drugs or alcohol.

Teen Daughter: I hope so too, but this stuff is so hard to even think about.

Dad: It is. I'll give you that. One other argument for a thoughtful approach to sex is the risk of pregnancy and sexually transmitted diseases or STDs. There is so much material to cover here—much more than we have time to talk about today. But one general "rule" is to always, ALWAYS use a condom for anything that comes close to sexual intercourse. You simply can't know what STDs your partner is carrying, and a condom, though not foolproof, offers some reasonable protection. You should make a commitment to yourself that you will never have sex without a condom until you know you want to get pregnant.

Teen Daughter: Well, I do have one kind of embarrassing question. What if we decide we want to do some stuff but not go all the way? Is there any way to be sure that things stop before they go too far?

Dad: I've heard of one trick you could use. If you want to stay a virgin but are being sexual in other ways, take turns keeping your pants on. One thing that's for certain: you cannot have sexual intercourse if one person has his or her pants on with the fly closed.

Teen Daughter: That's an interesting idea...ugh, this all is so embarrassing.

Dad: Sorry, but this is all good to talk about. Let's jump to another topic: location. While it seems like a mundane thought, the location where sexual activity occurs is important to consider. The classic back seat of a car will be uncomfortable and potentially embarrassing or dangerous. One of my friends and his girlfriend were caught by the police on a golf course putting green...naked.

Teen Daughter: Wow, I think I'd die of embarrassment.

Dad: Reading about it in the newspaper would be a close second. I guess I'm trying to say that the importance of location is another argument for a thoughtful approach to sex. Since sex is a grown up thing to do, act like a grown up and treat sex like a grown up activity.

Teen Daughter: Ok, I hear you. Are we done now?

Dad: Just one more thing, let's talk about consent. Rape is such a common occurrence for college students, and it is often alcohol driven, that many colleges are trying to teach students what consent means. Here's how I think about it, both parties must consent at each increased level of sexual activity...and consent can't be given if the person is drunk or high.

Teen Daughter: We learned about contracts in one of my classes, so it's kind of like a contract, isn't it?

Dad: Exactly. The contract isn't valid unless both parties agree, and not under duress or while in an impaired state. I think that's enough for today. Thank you for putting up with my bumbling attempts to work through this stuff with you. You know your mother and I love you and treasure you and that you can always ask us anything. We promise to always try to hide our horror.

Teen Daughter: Ok, Dad. Thanks. Love you too.

Chapter 13

Keeping it Up: Sex through the Ages

My Dad tells the story of being on a ship in WWII. The first mate woke the sailors every morning by yelling that when they got old like him, a good bowel movement would feel better than coitus (he used more vivid words, but that's the gist).

When I was in my mid-30s, a friend in his mid-40s told me that by 40 I wouldn't care about sex any more. He said that part of life just sort of goes away. I remember thinking, "Man, I hope not!"

Fortunately, I'm in my 60s now and neither of those predictions has come true. Sex remains an important aspect of my life and is in many ways better than it ever was.

As I think back, I remember working as a roadie on rock and roll tours to pay my way through college. We were unloading a truck in Milwaukee and an old stagehand said, "You young guys just lather them up. It takes an old guy to finish them off." This mildly crude comment makes me happier as each year passes.

Your sex life will change throughout different stages of life. Let's look at some of the sex stages. We can look back with the ghost of coitus past or look ahead with the ghost of "getting-laid-future." Wise people try to understand the continuum.

Early Marriage

Maybe you had a big, fancy wedding, or perhaps you just went to the courthouse and picked up your marriage license. One way or the other, you've gotten yourself married to a whole other person...a person you thought you knew and adored.

Then the reality of married life strikes. This spouse you've promised yourself to until death lives like a slob. In fact, he or she *is* a slob. Or wants sex all the time, constantly, like three times a week. Or never wants to have sex, is always tired, and it only happens like two times a week. Or your spouse perpetrates various other offences that annoy you.

There is little that can prepare us for marriage. Humans seem to put their best behavior forward during courtship (even if it involves living together) but drop the charade after marriage. We all do it, so don't be surprised if your spouse did it to you. Don't focus on how your spouse changed and the resulting disappointment. The only effective action is to strive to forgive. It will be the best thing you can do with your early marriage years.

The other best thing you can do in your early years of marriage is to work toward agape love. Strive to love your spouse regardless of his or her behavior. To love with agape love is an act of will—a demonstration of character—but it's not just a sappy, "taking whatever comes" type of love.

M. Scott Peck defined love as "to judicially give and judicially withhold." This thoughtful and faithful agape love doesn't allow abuse. It loves deeply. It sees someone as God intended them to be seen.

Learning to love and forgive your spouse will be a lifelong challenge, but it is never more challenging than in the early marriage years. Let's consider how this may work in your sex life. One of you likely wants sex more often than the other. One will be pushing and one will be resisting. If you both strive to put aside your own strong desires and accommodate your partner, you'll grow as a couple. You'll build character.

During this time, the "How often do we have sex?" struggle can be combined with "No kids, minimal worries, lots of energy, our sex life will never be better than this, right?" And that can morph to, "You mean this is as good as sex will be...forever?"

That thinking puts unnecessary stress on sex levels. Think of the lie so many teenagers hear, that "these are the best years of your life." That simple lie creates so much depression among young people. Were your teenage years the best of your life? I hope not.

You likely recall some fond memories and perhaps long for less responsibility in your life, but think of all the wisdom you've gained since then. Think about how much more you know about love and about God. If we strive to grow more Christ-like each year, we understand the lie that the best years are the early ones.

Another thing to consider during the early marriage years is the likelihood that your sex is enthusiastic but perhaps not satisfying for your partner. It takes lots of trust, communication, and practice to figure out what curls your spouse's toes.

Many couples don't get to this level of sexual satisfaction until their 40s or 50s. Some never get there. Do what you can to connect earlier and better. If you're going to be spending all that time having sex with each other, why not seek to understand your partner and what they like and don't like?

If things really aren't going well in your sex life, please go to your doctor together. Write down your questions. Write down your problems, struggles, or concerns. If you're too embarrassed to talk, just hand the doctor your lists and respond to his or her questions.

Learn to look at your early marriage struggles through the lens of growing more Christ-like—your lifelong project. Your early marriage years give you a great opportunity to try, fail, forgive, ask for forgiveness, and try again.

The Baby Wars

Then God may show his sense of humor by throwing a baby into the mix. If you're fortunate enough to have babies, you will have a major upheaval in your sex life. God repurposes the woman's recreational and waste disposal area to grow another human. Soon after you conceive the little nipper, the changes start, bringing about wonderful and dreadful consequences.

Sex during pregnancy can go from little change (other than morning sickness) to some logistical challenges (i.e., how to work around a beach ball-sized protrusion under her shirt). Mood swings for a pregnant woman vary from minor to scary. Sexual desire can go from none to greatly increased.[162]

You'll both be running that gauntlet without an instruction manual. Pay attention to the "I feel fat" vs "I feel beautiful" matrix. It varies from woman to woman and from day to day. Husbands should show some extra love and kindness here. This is only one of many things going on during pregnancy. Here are a few others:

1. **Female genitals swell around the fourth month**, which often produces constant lubrication and sometimes more desire for sex.

2. **You can't get pregnant...you already are.**

---

[162] Paul Joannides, *Guide to Getting It On: A Book About the Wonders of Sex* (Oregon: Goofy Foot Press, 2014), 805-822.

3. **Female orgasms can be more intense** (and multiple).

4. **Male orgasms may also be more intense** due to swelling female genitals (and the increased level of love that's developing in you).

5. **Breast tenderness may occur**. Men should "Wax On, Wax Off" with coconut oil.

6. When the man wants sex and the woman doesn't, the man should consider **"Waxing Off"** in a different way.

7. **Get a zippered mattress encasement** to ease concerns about leaking urine and other fluids. It protects against bed bugs as well, so just do it.[163]

8. **Don't worry about hurting or annoying the baby**, he or she will have plenty of years to get back at you.

9. **If your doctor does tell you to refrain from sex**, ask why, for how long, and what's included in prohibited sex. You get the health care you accept.

10. **Pay attention if the soon-to-be Mom** wants more touch or less touch during pregnancy (and what kind of touch). Perhaps she will

---

[163] I recently bought some at Amazon for about $40. Search "zippered mattress encasement."

want less intercourse but more romantic touching. Or she may desire to masturbate more. Or it could be something completely different. Just pay attention to touch needs and wants.

Then the baby arrives. Wow! You really didn't believe it actually worked like that, did you? Try to bond during this amazing experience, as plenty of stress to your bond will hit you soon. For example, consider having sex after the baby. Generally, a woman's libido drops to record lows right after giving birth. Unfortunately, this doesn't usually happen to men. Lack of sleep may also play a major role in sexual negotiations.

This time in life, which can last years, often becomes sexually stressful for both spouses. You're tired and you often don't like each other...and sometimes you're not so sure about the baby. Don't freak out about it. Most folks have gone through it without ending up in jail, and you can too. One tip that will help you succeed in the baby wars is to talk about sex before the little tax deduction arrives.[164] Here are some questions you could ask each other:

1. What do you think our sex life will be like right after the baby is born?
2. How about a few months in?
3. What do you think our new normal will become?
4. What do you want it to become?
5. What if the baby is colicky or I get postpartum depression?[165]
6. Her: What if you see me as a mother instead of a lover and aren't interested in me? What if I look different?
7. Him: What if I'm ready for action and I feel guilty asking you because I don't want to put you on the spot?

By the way, a good answer to this last one may be that we agree for this special time that it's always ok for the more sexed-up partner to ask and ok for the

---

[164] Paul Joannides, *Guide to Getting It On: A Book About the Wonders of Sex* (Oregon: Goofy Foot Press, 2014), p. 819

[165] Here are two excellent books to help you with those challenges: *Love in the Time of Colic* by Ian Kerner and Heidi Raykeil, and *After the Stork: The Couples Guide to Preventing and Over-Coming PostPartum Depression* by Sara Rosenquist.

less sexed-up partner to say no. Learn to think of a trip to the shower as part of the Fruits of the Spirit.

Finally, make a plan to get out on a date on a regular schedule. If you don't plan, it won't happen. Keeping your friendship and romantic love alive will bless your baby more than anything else you do.

The Teen Wars

The early school years aren't simple, but they tend to be a breathing break between the baby years and the teen years. As your children struggle to become adults—or independent at the least—you will encounter conflict. The more that conflict bothers you, the more it will affect your sex life. Hopefully you and your spouse learned to work together as a team when the kids were young. Kids are masters of the "divide and conquer" strategy. Parents need to hang tough as a team, even when one spouse says something that drives the other crazy.

Debby and I found parenting in the teen years a tremendous challenge, but God used this time to help us draw closer. This "us against them" time made us stronger as a couple. We loved raising our kids and thought we'd hate when they left home. The teen wars helped with that. By the time they were ready to leave, we were ready for them to be someplace other than home. We actually looked forward to having an empty nest.

When the Chicks Fly the Coop

When our last child left home, we found energy to reconnect in a much less stressful manner. We took the time to learn to enjoy each other again without the constant stress of teenagers. We started building the foundation for the rest of our lives together.

But some folks divorce soon after their kids leave home. What drives one couple one way or the other? Look at your relationship trend through the baby and teen wars. Have you been getting closer as you worked as a team through the struggles, or have you split the tasks and drifted apart?

When the last kid leaves, are you waking up the next day with someone you don't like very much or with your best friend? If you're waking next to your best friend, you're going to love the empty nest, and more adventuresome sex can follow more available time and energy.

On the other hand, if you wake up with someone you don't like, you need to take up a realistic view. There has probably been a process of withdrawal on the one side and ignoring the withdrawal on the other. Many couples now divorce after 50, often around the time the kids leave. Unfortunately, it often takes one spouse by almost complete surprise.

Planning can help prevent this ugly surprise. A few years before you'll reach the empty nest, initiate conversations about what you want your "no kids at home" life to be. Just like business planning, make a strategic plan for your marriage future. Discuss your marriage strengths, weaknesses, opportunities, and threats. Dream about what you'd like to have and do with each other. Make an action plan that moves you in the right direction.

Make sure that action plan includes spending time together as a couple. Even if you find you talk about the kids most of the time, get in the habit of spending regular and special time together. Consider the emotional and financial costs of divorce; work to avoid it if both parties are willing to try. As my accountant says, "Divorce is too difficult and costly; it's better one of you should die."

Moving Toward the Sunset

Unlike a real sunset, no one knows when our light will extinguish. We can decide, however, to live vigorously until that time comes. We can keep having great sex in our 50s, 60s, 70s, 80s, and 90s. I don't know much about post-centenarian sex. Send me a note if you do (you'll be one of my heroes).

Here are a few "Sex for old-folks" tips:

1. **Let go of expectations**. Don't focus on how things were years ago. Enjoy what you are and can do right in this moment.
2. **Strive to be honest**. It's sexy, and at your age you're not going to be so good at remembering lies.
3. **Protect yourself from sexually transmitted diseases**. Pregnancy scares may be in the past, but STDs are ever present. Take the time to learn how to have safe sex.
4. **Focus on physical touch and intimacy**. You have time. Use it to enjoy each other deeply. Don't make it all about intercourse. Include baths, massage, talking, playing, maybe even wrestling. Just avoid Ultimate Fighting.
5. **Lube, lube, lube** (and yoga, yoga, yoga for flexibility)
6. **Watch your back (and knees).** Aging reduces the utility of joints. Try spooning instead of doggie style to put less stress on your back and knees. The lap dance position (man sitting on a chair and woman sitting on

his lap facing him) also yields fun sex with little body stress.

7. **Think beyond intercourse**. Try mutual masturbation with some oral sex thrown in. Or try 69. Or maybe try 68 (you do me and I'll owe you one). Whatever it takes.

8. If you just aren't getting that "off to the races" feeling about sex anymore, **revisit chapter 5, "Aphrodisiacs: Who-aaaah!"** You may find something there that stokes your fire. I don't want to be the pusher man, but cannabis can have an amazing and immediate effect on your libido.

9. **Give each other foot massages regularly.** Geriatricians stress the importance of proper foot function. Falls are one of the main risks of aging, and functional feet help prevent falls. If you have some kind of foot phobia, get over it. You don't have that much time left.

10. Finally, if you are having a physical problem with sex (e.g., erectile dysfunction for men or painful sex for women), **don't ignore it.** Many medications have side effects that muck up sex; work to find medications that don't. Don't be embarrassed to talk with your doctor. He or she has recently had a finger

inside you, so assume you are on intimate enough terms to ask questions about sex.

I hope the tips above encourage you to keep at sex as long as you live. Orgasms are good for you. Don't give them up.

Spiritual Conclusion: How to Live

The more you love God, the more struggles you're likely to have. Think about the hard times Paul, Timothy, Joseph, and, the best example, Jesus went through. But full commitment also brings the most joy. I love the analogy of walking along a railroad track: our entire life, we will have a suffering track on one side and a joy track on the other.

As we walk through our life, sex can be one of our great joys. It can also cause unrivaled suffering. We've spent most of this book trying to find the joy in sex. Let's end by thinking about how to morph that great sex life into a life fully committed to Christ.

Schmucks and Menschs of the Bible

The Bible is God's love story to us. Look at all the ways God shows his love to the various characters in the biblical story and tells us to love each other. Getting this love stuff right is one of the main purposes of life. How do we learn to love from the Bible?

Let's start with "good guys" and "bad guys" in the biblical stories. We'll call the good guys *Menschs* (a person of integrity and honor), and the bad guys are *Schmucks* (a foolish or contemptible person). Who are some of Schmucks of the Bible? Jesus spent much of his time telling the religious leaders and Pharisees they were schmucks. Here are some others:

1. The other guy on the cross that didn't end up in heaven that day.
2. The two busy guys in the Good Samaritan story
3. Solomon's son Rehoboam
4. Saul, the first king of Israel
5. Ahab and all the evil kings of Israel

What do all these schmucks have in common? They are arrogant and entitled (i.e., anything but humble). They act as if they have all the answers. They are self-important, valuing themselves way above others. They are not kind.

I'd call them blowhard know-it-alls. I hate spending time with folks like that. I have to be careful not to become one.

Now let's look at the Menschs: Jesus, Paul, Timothy, Abraham, Joseph, Moses, David, Jonathan, Ruth, Esther, Job, and many more. What differentiates them? They all have humility. They take life as it comes and try to follow God's direction. A thread of kindness runs through all of them, though many showed incredible strength with that kindness. These Menschs were courageous. They handled their struggles with integrity and honor.

When I contemplate how I want to behave or what I want to believe, this clear choice between Schmuck and Mensch behavior helps me decide what to do in any given situation. It is like the "What Would Jesus Do?" concept, but it can be spread over to a few more folks who weren't the Son of God.

I like starting with the basic question, "Is this Jerk behavior?" Unfortunately, it's a question too many Christians never ask. Consider behaviors such as leaving a lousy tip at a restaurant (something Christians are known for), acting judgmental and self-righteous (another popular perception of Christians), or not being kind when it would be easy to do so.

Simply not being a jerk should be the starting point for Christians or for anyone striving to live a meaningful life, but effective Christian living needs to go much further than that.

Love and Forgiveness

Study the Gospels and you'll find that the most revolutionary teaching of Jesus was forgiveness. He told his followers they'd be forgiven as they forgive.[166] He told several parables about the importance of forgiveness.[167] While the Old Testament shows Joseph forgiving his brothers and David forgiving Mephibosheth, these acts are simply noted as the character of a good man.[168] Jesus makes forgiveness a crucial part of loving God and loving others.

I've found the best way to live forgiveness every day is to let go of attachments. I'm not the general manager of the Universe; I need to let go of that attachment of wanting to boss others around and "help" them. I let go of the attachment of thinking I deserve to be treated a certain way, with the amount of respect due a man of my position.

I strive to remember how much respect Jesus and Paul received from those who opposed them, and realize I deserve much less than I get. As I struggle to give up entitlement and embrace humility, forgiveness flows naturally. And when I muck it up, I promptly forgive myself and try again to forgive others.

---

[166] Matthew 6:14-15, Mark 11:25-26

[167] Parable of the unforgiving servant, Matthew 18:21-35. Parable of Brother Who Sins Against You, Matthew 18:15-20. Parable of the Prodigal Son, Luke 15:11-32. Story of the woman taken in adultery, John 8:1-11.

[168] Genesis 50:19-21 (entire story goes from Genesis 37 to 50); II Samuel 9

Letting go of attachments is central to forgiveness. Otherwise, forgiveness becomes just an act of will for something that we don't really believe. But when we let go of the attachment of what we deserve and who we are, we realize the truth of needing and offering forgiveness.

We embrace the reality that we don't have all the answers—that we are simply a life saved by Christ, struggling to love God and others. When Jesus tells his disciples they must hate their families, he is telling them to give up the attachment to anything on Earth (even though it may be a good and important thing) in order to love God entirely.[169]

The story of Job illustrates it best. Job lost his wealth, all his children were killed, he suffered with painful boils all over his body, he sat in grief for days, and then his friends told him it all had to be his fault because a righteous God wouldn't allow this to happen to a good man. Yet Job continued to love God, even in anger about his circumstances.

Part of my daily prayers include what I call "Job's prayer."

> *Lord, I give you my possessions,*
> *My relationships,*
> *My health,*
> *My time,*

---

169 Luke 14:25-34

My reputation
And my life.

I often shudder after saying "My relationships," as I consider losing my children and grandchildren and so many others that I deeply love. But I know my love for God must be higher than all that. That's what I think it means to hate your family in order to love God.

As I strive to live in that deep love with God, I realize I need to let go of resentment, but I can't. Then I remember God doesn't ask me to change my feelings; he asks me to forgive. When I make that choice to forgive, my feelings follow along behind, usually later and sporadically.

While God doesn't ask us to change our feelings, he does ask us to change our actions. God can heal every wound, but we need to choose to forgive to let the healing begin. Jesus taught this revolutionary concept in a way that was pertinent in ancient times, the Middle Ages, the Renaissance, whatever crazy times we now brave, and every future time.

My Sex: Celebration or Sin?

As I love God and love others, as I strive to let go of attachments and to forgive others, how do I honor God with my sex life? How do I determine what is joyful sex and what is sinful sex? Start by defining sin. A traditional understanding is that the Bible stipulates sinful actions. Murder, adultery, lying, and stealing are sins.

But God is a God of complexity. Was Dietrich Bonhoeffer committing sin as he helped plot the murder of Adolf Hitler? Bonhoeffer was killed for these efforts and most folks would say he was a courageous man who was attempting to follow the Holy Spirit's direction in his life.

Many church leaders in early Nazi Germany meekly followed the law and their leaders. These folks reaped the benefits of acquiescence. They were rewarded by Hitler for their loyalty. Looking through the lens of history, we despise those cowards. To stay in that historical time, the civilian Germans who hid Jews and lied when the Nazis came looking for them lied with honor. No one would call that courageous behavior sinful.

Could adultery ever not be sinful? Consider a woman who cares for her husband with dementia for many years. She works at a job, acts as primary caregiver, and lives in brutal loneliness. If she falls in love with another man, may she act on that passion? Some would say, "God makes life hard. She just has to follow the rules." Others would see some room for grace in that scenario.

Perhaps we should start with the premise that sin has victims. Murder, stealing, and child molesting all have clear victims. Putting anything higher than God (idolatry, greed, immorality, etc.) makes God and ourselves the victim. We evaluate the sinfulness of a behavior partly by the harm the sinful act causes.

We also consider intent. Sinful behavior tends to have selfish, lazy, or unkind intent. Good behavior tends to be done in a loving manner, and it often requires extra effort.

For example: is masturbation sinful? Consider a scenario in which the wife had a baby several months ago and is feeling overwhelmed, exhausted, and anti-sexy. The husband still has his normal sex drive. It seems to me that the husband letting his wife sleep and heading to the shower to shake hands with the Admiral can be considered an act of compassion.

On the other hand, frequent self-gratification could make masturbation an idol in a person's life. If important things go undone because you put so much time and effort into pleasing yourself, victims emerge. Also, if the intent is selfish and lazy, it may be sinful.

By the way, if a behavior simply creeps you out, you are not victimized by that behavior. You may feel uncomfortable with the thought of men having sex with other men, but that doesn't make you a victim, and it doesn't make gay sex sinful.

Are there *any* rules for sex?

1. **Any non-consensual sex (read *rape*) is sin.** When a husband forces his wife to have sex with him, when unwanted sexual activity happens on a date, or when a person is unable to give consent, any sexual action is rape.
2. **Any sex with a child is sin.** Child molestation seems the most egregious sin fallen humanity has devised.
3. **Sex that violates a trust (such as adultery) is sin.** Solomon describes a foolish young man seduced by a married woman as sin with consequences.[170] Godly sex should not create victims. This concept covers the two words (*Pornea* and *Moichos*) the Bible uses for prohibited sex.[171]

As you consider what to do or not do in your own sex life, think about doing what you can to make God smile. He loves you more than you can imagine (unless you have grandchildren, then you might have a limited idea of that kind of love). Make your sex a celebration. Act with love and make the effort to have *Great Sex, Christian-Style*.

Living the Fruits

We discussed the Fruits of the Spirit (love, joy, peace, patience, kindness, goodness, gentleness, and

---

[170] Proverbs 7
[171] See page 147 for definitions of Pornea and Moichos.

self-control) in chapter 5. [172] Living the Fruits of the Spirit will make you desirable to your spouse. God seems to share this view.

I fully believe that we can never behave in a way that is acceptable to God without the grace of Jesus, but I also know that Jesus said, "By their fruits you will recognize them [as believers]." [173] Jesus also told his followers that they had no part in him if they didn't live in love.[174]

While I strive to refrain from judging others, I can't live in society without making some guesses about who can and can't be trusted. When I see Christians living the Fruits of the Spirit, I tend to believe their profession of faith. But when I see professing Christians who aren't living those fruits, I doubt their sincerity.

I've often been guilty of living a fruitless life. In our early years of marriage, I often annoyed Debby with my thoughtlessness and selfishness. A wise friend lived with us for a couple of years, and he gave me some advice: "Ned, when you're in any kind of conflict with Debby, think about the thing you want to do next, then do the opposite."

---

[172] Galatians 5:22-23
[173] Matthew 7:16
[174] Matthew 7:23

I initially assumed this was just another way for him to tell me I was a moron, but when I tried to follow his advice, it often worked. If I wanted to respond in anger, I instead said something nice. If I wanted to walk away, I stayed. If I wanted to agree just to get it over with, I instead tried harder to understand.

Over the years, I've found this technique consistently helpful. The practice forces me to stop and think, and that may be the biggest benefit. I take myself off automatic pilot and consider who I am, who she is, and our relationship with each other and God. The technique is like anti-jerk spray.

Living intentionally in this one moment is the best way to live. Being aware of the Fruits of the Spirit helps us live well, but we need to guard against making it our primary focus, making our spouse the focus, or making great sex the focus. Loving God must be our focus. When we focus on loving God, we naturally love others.

Sex Conclusion: Recipe for Making Love

Do you ever ponder why God gave us sex? He designed this amazingly intimate activity that we do regularly for our entire lives (if we're lucky). It seems to me that sex is a special intersection where the spiritual meets the physical. The previous chapter covered the spiritual, now let's look at one practical recipe for the physical.

1. **The "Before You Start" List**:
   a. Clean yourself. Pheromones are nice, but funky smells repel. Clean every area that may be dirty, including armpits, genitals, butt, feet, ears, mouth, etc.
   b. Consider shaving. Bristly hair feels like sandpaper.
   c. Perform fingernail and toenail maintenance. Remember that scene in *Dumb and Dumber* where they use an industrial high speed grinder to trim the toenails? Funny; not sexy. Make sure your nails are clean, trimmed, and smooth.

     d. Consider applying perfume or cologne. Go light here, though, as your lover will hopefully soon be licking those locations, and those products aren't designed to taste good. Some natural essential oils (peppermint, vanilla, or lavender) can be wonderful for smell and taste.

     e. Set the mood with low lighting, candles, flowers, and whatever beauty you can create.

2. **A Recipe for Lovemaking**:

     a. Massage her body over her clothes. Pay attention to her back, neck, and scalp.

     b. Transition to kissing. Have a nice make-out session. Take off shirts as kissing moves down to chests, torsos, and backs.

     c. Go back to massaging her, with a massage oil candle burning nearby. Put some of that hot oil on her back and give a good, deep-tissue back massage. Work up around her neck and scalp.

     d. As you are massaging, work your way down to her butt and take off her pants. Use that oil to massage each leg and foot.

e. Have her turn over and start massaging her feet with massage oil. Massage up her legs, hips, belly, breasts, shoulders, neck, and face. Don't linger on her private parts here; show some restraint, man!

f. After some more kissing, let her take the lead. Kiss his neck, chest, belly, around the pubic area, thighs, balls, and finally work up to the penis. Don't go to orgasm here, just work him up close to the edge, then transition to something else that feels good, but not quite that good.

g. Now some more kissing and hugging and just rubbing your naked bodies against each other, rolling around into different positions.

h. With him on top, look deeply into each other's eyes and slowly slide the penis into the vagina. Don't pound away for orgasm here, just slowly move in and out. See if he can ride up a bit higher and rub his penis against her clitoris. As he gets to the edge of orgasm, pull out and start just kissing.

i. Then kiss and fondle down her neck, breasts, stomach and to the vulva.

j. Perform cunnilingus slowly and with love. Bring her to orgasm.

k. Then come back into the missionary position and finish.

I offer this recipe to illustrate the give and take of one beautiful love making session. Use your creativity and your love to satisfy each other in your own unique ways. And remember, it's good to giggle in bed, just don't point and giggle.

Acknowledgements

I'm grateful Lex Pelger, Claire Berjot, Anna Pelger-DiCicco, Chris DiCicco and Tessa Pelger could mostly get past the "Ewww" factor about their parents having sex and help in so many ways with this book.

Also, the following folks read drafts or gave comments that shaped my writing: Tim Barley, Sr, Matt Bieber, Mike Bingeman, Bob and Geneva Brandt, Theresa Brown, Evelyn Epstein, Jill and Shawn Erb, Scott Fetteroff, Ron Fox, D.W. Gregory, E.E. Griffith, Boris and Tatjana Kalabra, Penn Ketchum, Howard and Sue Kramer, Dragan Lalovic, Brandy and Kneal Leininger, Lisa and Philip Lorish, Mike Mountz, Jay Polansky, Ben Samberg, Erik and Jackie Schouten, Jason Shaeffer, Jim Singer, Stacy Smith, Beth and Bruce Spicer, Dave and Robin Stieber, Diane and Scott Stieber, Melody Strayer, Jim and Lisa Stuckey, Dave Wiedis, Dave Williams, and J.D. Young.

Kathrin Herr, The Writing Mechanic, edited, prodded and created with skill and grace. She made this book production process a pleasure and gets my highest recommendation.

Please understand that acknowledgement here in no way means agreement with anything I've written. The folks listed were loving enough to help a poor sinner searching for truth (and a few laughs).

Scriptural Index

General Index

About the Author

Ned Pelger, PE loves God, Debby, kids, grandkids, a big extended family and more friends than anyone deserves.

He strives to live with joy and purpose in every area of his life—and to eat a piece of good chocolate every day. Ned previously wrote *Joyful Living: Build Yourself a Great Life!*

See GreatSexChristianStyle.com or Pelger.com for more info.

Made in the USA
San Bernardino, CA
02 March 2019